first crack
your egg!

John Burton Race & Angela Hartnett

first crack your egg!

photography by Peter Cassidy

Quadrille

The star rating for each recipe in
the book indicates degree of difficulty:

✳ = easy

✳✳ = medium

✳✳✳ = advanced

contents

introduction

As restaurateurs, we both have considerable experience in training up young chefs – but taking on would-be cooks with absolutely no experience and teaching them to cook to chef standard in a matter of weeks, as we did recently, was quite another kind of challenge!

In the end, though, one of our abiding principles is that good cooking begins with the simplest of recipes and the most basic of techniques, so we've started our cookery course with the humble egg. By the time you've learnt how to cook an egg properly you have acquired several fundamentals of good cooking, such as proper appreciation of your ingredients and the importance of timing. After that, you're well on your way to being able to cook.

More than anything, we want anyone who follows this course to realise that food, cooking and eating are fun, not a chore. We've included dishes from many different countries and traditions – Italian, French, British, Indian, Thai, to name but a few – because this is the way all of us eat today and therefore what we want to be able to cook.

We have included detailed steps in words and pictures for each of the most useful techniques you are liable to need, and provided as many hints, tips, variations and extra ideas as we can, so you really feel you have one of us standing by your side as you attempt each recipe.

Each dish is clearly labelled with one, two or three stars showing you the level of difficulty. Our hope is that you will get great enjoyment and satisfaction learning and working your way from one to two to three-star dishes.

Angela Hartnett
John Burton Race

cooking kit

Chopping boards

It doesn't really matter whether your chopping board is wood or plastic from a health perspective. What's important is that it is solid and resolutely stays still on your worktop while you are using it - the chefs' trick for guaranteeing this is to lay a damp cloth underneath it. Also essential is to clean it thoroughly, especially after you've been cutting up raw poultry, meat or fish. Consider keeping a separate chopping board for vegetables and fruit.

General kitchen knife

This small, pointed knife about 9-10cm long will be one of the ones you use most. It's designed for cutting work that requires more control than chopping: scoring tomatoes, peeling apples, topping and tailing vegetables.

Chopping knife

A knife you will use every day, the chopping knife has a narrow point and a wide heel and a blade about 20cm long. In general, the best ones are the heaviest.

Fish knife

Fish knives look similar to chopping knives but their blade is much finer and more flexible. This allows it to bend into the skeleton of the fish and remove the maximum amount of flesh from the bone.

Palette knife

A palette knife is more versatile than a fish slice. In addition to being great for turning foods and removing them from the frying pan, it will help move delicate items or anything requiring careful handling, such as a cake.

Carving knife

A chopping knife is not a good substitute for a carving knife as its heel is too thick and will give uneven slices. For carving you need a dedicated long-bladed knife that allows you to keep your back straight and forearm rigid while cutting. For thin, even slices, use the whole length of the blade and drag it through the meat in one long, continuous movement, applying very little pressure.

Bread knife

The knife you use for bread should be serrated or have pointed teeth so you can use it like a saw with very little pressure. Flat-bladed knives demand that you push them through the bread, which will ruin the shape of the loaf.

Cleaver

Cleavers are used for chopping poultry and meat bones. A small one will do, about 12.5cm long and 5cm deep. Alternatively you can use a very heavy, large chopping knife with a thick heel (don't use a small one as the bones could damage the blade). When using a cleaver, apply the pressure at the base of the blade, near the handle.

Knife sharpener

It sounds contradictory, but sharp knives are safer to use than blunt ones. Sharp knives cut cleanly through ingredients, while blunt ones force you to apply pressure that can cause slips. Professional chefs regularly use steels to sharpen their knives, but steels demand proper technique that needs to be learned. In the domestic scenario, use whatever sharpener you feel comfortable with - you might like to try a chantry sharpener that simply requires you to run the blade through the gadget's guide.

Peeler

There are a variety of peelers on the market. Use the one you feel comfortable with. A good option is a double-bladed 'speed' peeler that allows you to peel in both directions, and therefore peel your vegetables twice as quickly.

Saucepans

Before you buy saucepans check they are suitable for your cooktop - the store will be able to tell you. Gas hobs and high heats demand pans with thick bases to ensure they conduct heat well, while pans for induction hobs need to have completely flat bases and a certain composition. The most useful sizes to buy are 15 and 20cm. You'll be using them everyday, so it's worth spending money on quality.

Pots and casseroles

These large pans tend to be used for dishes like stocks, soups and stews needing long cooking over a low heat, so choose models with a heavy base that will retain heat efficiently. However, it is also essential that you feel comfortable picking it up when it is full of ingredients.

Obviously you don't need all this stuff to begin with. Start with a couple of good knives, a sturdy pair of scissors and a flexible spatula. A couple of deep saucepans (one large), a heavy frying pan and an omelette pan, and you're there.

Frying pans

It may sound crazy, but you should always buy frying pans that will fit in your oven and have ovenproof handles. This allows you to sear meat over a high heat on the hob then transfer it to the oven to finish cooking without having to get out a baking tray. It saves on washing up too. For daily use you should also have a small frying pan; a non-stick one is ideal for egg dishes.

Wok

A wok is specifically designed for stir-frying and has the optimum shape for the job, but unless you plan to cook a lot of traditional stir-fried dishes it is not essential. If you do want to buy one, go for a single-handled design which is easiest to control while stir-frying.

Baking sheets and trays

Check the internal dimensions of your oven before buying these as they need to fit inside it and allow enough room for proper heat circulation. A completely flat baking sheet is indispensable for baking and cooking en papillote (in a bag), and doubles as a handy flat surface for chocolate work.

Scales

A family of four is unlikely to need a set of scales with a capacity greater than 2.25kg, so there is no need to buy a larger, more expensive set. It's handy if they can weigh in imperial as well as metric measures, so that you can use recipes from old cookbooks, but otherwise the controls should be as simple as possible. Look for one with a stainless steel pan for durability and to prevent flavour transference of ingredients.

Sieves

Most domestic sieves are border-line-useless as the mesh is not fine enough. It is better to spend £12-15 on one conical cross-meshed professional model than to have an array of sieves hanging around the kitchen.

Balloon whisk

Whisks are used for emulsifying and whipping air into ingredients. Choosing a fine one with as many strands as possible will minimise the pressure on your wrist. Go for an elongated (rather than round) balloon shape about 22-26cm long.

Wooden spoons

Indispensable. There's nothing wrong with the plastic equivalents - both materials have a tendency to dry out, crack and absorb flavours to some extent. Dedicate one to pungent savoury ingredients such as onion and garlic.

Tongs

Chefs have stainless steel or aluminium tongs for turning things such as steaks over and removing them from the griddle or pan.

Ladle

Not just for serving soups and sauces, ladles are wonderful for skimming stocks. Make sure you don't get one too big for your saucepans. Small ones are easy to control when you are putting sauce on a plate.

Rubber spatula

Rubber spatulas allow you to run right around the edge of bowls when making things such as cakes and mayonnaise, ensuring that you don't waste ten per cent of the mixture.

Rolling pin

The best rolling pin is the one you feel comfortable using. Many people find they prefer the type without handles.

Ramekins

Choose ovenproof ramekins that have a capacity of 250-300ml. Straight-sided porcelain models are preferable to metal or Pyrex.

Apron

An apron is not just to help keep your clothes clean, it protects you from burns and spillages and ensures you cook hygienically. You need one that's easy to pull off quickly with one hand, in case of an accident.

Pasta machine

Strictly speaking, you can roll pasta dough with a rolling pin and therefore do not need a dedicated machine. If pasta is your passion, it's worth investing in a large industrial model that allows you to roll a greater volume of pasta with the same amount of energy as the smaller machines. Of the small machines, the Imperial brand is a good choice.

Liquidizers, stick blenders and food processors

You do not need a portfolio of these machines, which are great for making soups, sauces and anything puréed. Stick blenders tend to be less durable than liquidizers and food processors but you have the advantage of being able to use them directly in the saucepan.

Electric mixer

Not just for cake making, electric mixers are good for whisking if you don't have a great deal of strength in your arms, and for making pastry when the paddle attachment is fitted. When using them to make mousses, make sure the bowl and whisk and perfectly clean and chill them before use.

Invest in the more elaborate and costly items as and when you can and need them. If you get into baking, you'll need a stout rolling pin, a couple of baking sheets and a wire cooling rack, then dishes and pans as you require them.

useful techniques

Dicing onions *is best done by first halving the onion through the root, then leaving the root intact, cutting each half several times up to the root. Holding the half tightly with the other hand, cut across these slices.*

Poaching *is taking place when only a few bubbles rise sporadically to the surface of the liquid. The pan is kept over a low heat or in some cases removed from the heat altogether once the water is bubbling.*

Simmering *is required for food that needs to be cooked slowly and evenly, such as potatoes and soups. The ingredients are brought to a boil, then the heat is turned down so that the surface of the liquid is scattered with small bubbles.*

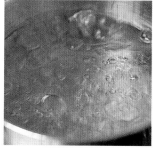 

Boiling *is used when food needs to be cooked quickly to retain colour, as with green vegetables, or so it doesn't stick together, as with pasta, etc. The pan is kept over a high or moderately high heat and bubbles appear continuously right across the surface.*

Sweating *vegetables, especially onions, is often required at the beginning of a dish. The vegetables are cooked in a little fat over a medium-high heat so that they release water and soften without colouring. Once the ingredients are hot, stir often to prevent the vegetables sticking to the base of the pan and starting to brown.*

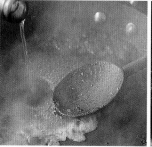 

Deglazing *is a method of incorporating the tasty caramelised cooking juices at the bottom of a pan into a sauce. A small amount of liquid, usually alcohol such as wine, is poured into the hot pan, where it will bubble and start to evaporate. You can help the sediment dissolve by stirring with a wooden spoon, or shaking the pan.*

Reducing *is means of thickening and intensifying the flavour of liquids, especially sauces. The liquid is boiled rapidly so water in the mixture evaporates and the total volume of liquid is reduced by, say, half. Sometimes cream is added to the reduced sauce and the mixture is brought to the boil and reduced again.*

Coating *consistency is achieved when a sauce is thick enough to coat the back of a spoon. To test it, run your finger through the sauce. It will be thin and pourable when the trail left by your finger slowly runs back together, and a thicker, clinging sauce when the trail remains clear.*

Blanching *is a means of part-cooking ingredients, especially vegetables; it is also used when peeling tomatoes. The ingredients are added to a large pan of rapidly boiling water and cooked briefly (from seconds to a few minutes, depending on ingredient and recipe). They are then lifted out and plunged into iced water to halt the cooking process and help preserve the colour.*

Segmenting *removes tough membranes from citrus fruit. With a very sharp knife, cut a slice from both top and bottom of the fruit, so the flesh is just revealed. Then (over a bowl to catch juices) cut down around the fruit, following its curve, so white pith and peel are removed. Cut down both sides of a segment as close to the membrane as possible, and ease segment out into the bowl.*

Separating eggs *allows you to use the yolks and whites in different ways. When the whites are to be whisked to a meringue, it is important there is no trace of yolk in them. Crack the egg on the side of a bowl and, holding it over the bowl, use your thumbs to ease the shell apart, allowing some of the white to slip into the bowl. Using the two halves of the shell like cups, gently pass the yolk between them, letting the rest of the white fall into the bowl. Put the yolk in a second bowl.*

Whisking egg whites *incorporates air into them, giving greater volume and foamy texture essential for soufflés and meringue. For best results, eggs should be a few days old and at room temperature. Whisk with an electric mixer or balloon whisk in a large, spotlessly clean bowl. The whites are at 'soft peak' stage when you hold the whisk up and the tips of the whites droop back down. 'Stiff peak' is when these stay upright. The terms are also applied to whipped cream.*

eggs & cheese

1

Who says you don't have the time to make a nutritious cooked breakfast? A boiled egg or two can take as little as three minutes to cook, once the water is bubbling, and with buttered toast and a sprinkling of salt and pepper they are absolutely delicious, says Angela. Other good reasons to nail this most basic of cooking skills: boiled eggs make a handy lunch when chopped to give egg mayonnaise sandwiches, and feature in smart niçoise salads.

boiled eggs

Per person
*1-2 medium eggs, at room
  temperature*

Tip
The term boiled egg is a misnomer. What you really want to do is simmer them, as the vigorous bubbling of boiling will encourage the shells to crack and the whites will then leak.

Fill a saucepan two-thirds full of water and bring it to the boil.

Using a slotted spoon, very carefully place the egg(s) in the pan and, as soon as the water starts to boil again, start timing the egg(s).

For a soft-boiled egg (with soft white and yolk) allow 3 minutes.

For an egg with a firm white but a soft yolk allow 5 minutes.

For a hard-boiled egg allow 10 minutes.

When ready, lift the egg(s) from the pan and allow to cool for a few minutes before serving. If you are hard-boiling eggs, then cool them fast in cold water to stop all cooking and prevent discoloration of the yolk.

Variation Quails' eggs are tiny so need to be boiled for just a minute for soft-boiled and 2-3 minutes for hard-boiled. Cook one first as a test to check your preferred timing.

Many dishes are claimed to be quick and easy but scrambled eggs really are. The correct texture is just set: the eggs shouldn't be cooked for so long they are rubbery enough to bounce off your shoe, says John. Remember that the mixture will continue cooking in the residual heat of the pan even after removal from the stove. A last-minute splash of cream helps halt that process.

scrambled eggs

Serves 1
3 eggs
2 tbsp double cream
20g butter
salt and pepper

Tip
The best scrambled egg texture is achieved by constant stirring. Don't stop to change the radio station or have a cigarette while they are cooking.

Crack the eggs into a mixing bowl. Add 1 tablespoon of the cream and whisk together.

Melt the butter in a heavy-based saucepan. Pour in the eggs and add some salt and pepper.

Cook over a gentle heat stirring constantly with a wooden spoon until the eggs are set but still moist – do not let them get dry and hard.

Remove the pan from the heat and stir in the second tablespoon of cream. Serve on hot buttered toast, or in tartlets.

Supper ready twenty minutes after you have walked into the kitchen? You don't need a microwave oven and a stash of ready-meals when you know how to make the French omelette and its Italian cousin frittata.

omelette

Serves 1
3 eggs
10g cold butter, diced
2 tsp oil
salt and pepper

Crack the eggs into a bowl and beat with a fork until smooth. Stir in the cold diced butter.

Heat a heavy non-stick frying pan over a high heat and add the oil.

Season the eggs with salt and pepper. When the oil is smoking-hot, pour them quickly into the pan.

Using a fork in a circular motion, move the contents of the pan round and round, while at the same time moving the pan back and forth across the heat. Allow the eggs to start coagulating.

Stop stirring and shaking the pan. Allow the eggs to form a light skin, then remove the pan from the heat.

Pick up the pan and tilt the handle upwards and away from you. At the same time, tap the handle of the pan so that the omelette move towards the opposite end of the pan.

Using the side of a fork, fold the omelette over to form a cigar shape.

Turn the pan over and tip the omelette on to a plate. Serve immediately.

broccoli frittata

Serves 2-3
250g Tenderstem or purple sprouting broccoli
salt and pepper
2 tsp olive oil
a little butter
3 large eggs
1 tsp chopped mixed herbs, such as tarragon, parsley and basil

Bring a large saucepan of salted water to the boil, add the broccoli and cook until just tender. Drain well.

Preheat the grill.

Heat the oil and butter in a frying pan. Add the broccoli and cook lightly for about a minute.

Meanwhile, beat the eggs together in a bowl. Pour them over the broccoli, then season with some salt and pepper, and sprinkle with the mixed herbs. Cook for 2 minutes.

Transfer the frying pan to the grill briefly to cook the top of the frittata.

Cut into wedges and serve immediately, or leave until cold.

The word florentine is used to describe a dish it usually indicates the presence of spinach, as is the case with this luxurious vegetarian alternative to the brunch favourite, eggs benedict. Learning to make the cheese-flavoured mornay sauce that cloaks the poached eggs will hold you in good stead later for producing dishes such as cheese soufflé and lasagne, as it is simply a variation of béchamel, says John.

poached eggs *florentine*

Serves 4
4 large eggs
50ml white wine vinegar or tarragon vinegar
500g spinach
olive oil

For the mornay sauce
1 clove
1 small onion, peeled
450ml milk
1/4 bay leaf
1 thyme sprig
pinch of freshly grated nutmeg
55g butter
55g plain flour, sieved
110g mature cheddar cheese, grated

Tip
The acidity in the vinegar helps coagulate or set the egg whites quickly, but be careful not to add too much: you do not want your poached eggs to taste like vinegar, even if it is tarragon-flavoured.

To make the béchamel sauce, stick the clove in the onion and place in a saucepan with the milk, bay leaf, thyme and grated nutmeg. Bring the milk up to the boil, then reduce the heat so that the milk simmers.

Meanwhile, in another saucepan, melt the butter over a moderate heat. Blend in the flour and allow to cook for a couple of minutes until the mixture (which is called a roux) begins to take on a little colour.

Gradually add the milk through a conical sieve (this will catch the flavourings), stirring well after each addition to give a smooth sauce.

Turn the heat to low and cook the sauce for approximately 30 minutes. (You can discard the onion, clove and bay leaf.)

Take the sauce off the heat and whisk in the cheese little by little. When it is completely incorporated and the sauce is smooth, cover with cling film and set aside until required.

Put a medium-sized saucepan of water on the stove, add the vinegar and bring to a simmer. Working one at a time, break the eggs into a cup. Use a spoon to create a small whirlpool in the water and drop the egg into it so that the white immediately envelops the yolk. Leave to poach for about 4 minutes or until the white is set and the yolk is still soft.

While the eggs are cooking, add a splash of olive oil to a large saucepan. Add the spinach and a little salt and freshly ground pepper. Cook over a moderate heat for a maximum of 2 minutes or until the spinach has just wilted.

Drain the spinach, squeezing out any excess liquid by pressing the spinach against the side of the pan with a spoon. Divide the spinach among large serving bowls and arrange so that the spinach covers the bottom of the bowl.

Preheat the grill.

Remove the eggs from the pan with a slotted spoon and, holding a clean tea towel in your other hand, gently turn them on to the tea towel to absorb the excess water.

Place the eggs on top of the spinach. Pour the mornay sauce over the top of the eggs. Put the plates under the hot grill just until the surface of the sauce is browned, then serve immediately.

For a fun evening with the kids, John recommends lining them up along the kitchen bench and knocking these crêpes out one by one for them to eat hot straight from the pan. You don't have to wait until Shrove Tuesday.

pancakes *with lemon and sugar*

30g butter
150g plain flour
3 eggs
500ml milk
vegetable oil
caster sugar, for sprinkling
2 lemons, cut in half

Slowly whisk the milk into the flour, being careful to work out any lumps. (Alternatively, you could beat the mixture thoroughly with a wooden spoon.) When all the milk is added, the batter should be as thin as cold oil.

In a small pan, melt the butter and continue cooking until it is frothy and nut-brown in colour. Meanwhile, sieve the flour into a mixing bowl and make a well in the centre. Crack in the eggs and use a whisk to gradually stir the flour into them to make a paste.

Whisk in the nut-brown butter. This will give a nutty flavour to the batter and will help prevent sticking when the pancakes are being cooked.

Pass the batter through a fine sieve and leave it to rest for 30 minutes before cooking. This allows the starch in the flour to swell, giving the pancakes a light texture.

Quickly rotate the pan up and around (extravagantly!) so that the mixture completely covers the base. Making sure that it is spread thinly will result in a nice light pancake.

When ready to cook, heat a heavy frying pan and wipe the inside with vegetable oil. When the pan is hot, add a small ladleful of batter.

Cook steadily until the underside is pale golden and is no longer stuck to the base of the pan. The top should be just set. Flip the pancake over with a palette knife and cook the other side.

Eat immediately, sprinkled with caster sugar and lemon juice, or set the pancake aside while you cook the rest of the batter. Layer the cooked pancakes with squares of greaseproof paper to prevent sticking, then fold them into quarters and reheat them in the microwave cooker before serving.

For lemon and orange pancakes, make as above but use 200g plain flour, 2 eggs and 200ml milk. Once the milk mixture has been combined with the flour, stir in 200ml lager, then the finely grated zest of one orange and one lemon, 10g caster sugar and a pinch of salt. Cook 30g butter to nut-brown, then stir it into the batter and leave it to rest for 10 minutes before frying.

Here good old eggy bread gets upgraded to a glamorous dessert with a boozy kick. The French call it pain perdu, meaning 'forgotten bread', because nine times out of ten it will be made with stale brioche, says John. The bread absorbs the egg, giving a luscious texture. Once you are confident making this version, experiment with other flavour combinations, such as bananas cooked with muscovado sugar, grated nutmeg and a splash of rum.

cinnamon & apple french toast

Serves 2
2 eggs
100ml full-fat milk
60g caster sugar
2 tsp ground cinnamon
2 slices brioche
1 apple
20g butter
20ml calvados

Tip
If you are cooking on a gas burner, you can tilt the pan briefly into the flame to set it alight. As long as there is only a small amount of alcohol in the pan, it will burn off quickly and not cause a problem.

In a wide bowl, whisk together the eggs, 30g caster sugar and a pinch of the cinnamon.

Soak the brioche in the egg mixture for a couple of minutes.

Peel the apple, cut it into quarters and remove the core. Cut each quarter into three slices.

In a mixing bowl, combine the remaining cinnamon with another 30g caster sugar and toss the apples until they are well coated.

Melt 10g butter in a non-stick frying pan, add the apples and allow to brown over a reasonably high heat. Turn and brown on the other side.

In a large non-stick frying pan, melt the remaining 10g butter. Carefully drain each slice of brioche and fry for about 2 minutes on each side, or until golden brown.

Drain the brioche on kitchen paper and position the slices on warm serving plates.

Pour the calvados over the hot apples and carefully flame it by lighting a taper and holding the flame over the pan to ignite the vapours, then let the flames subside. (Do *not* add more alcohol if the pan fails to catch light.) Spoon the apples and sauce over the brioche and serve.

Variation For simple french toast, whisk together 2 eggs, 300ml full-fat milk, and 25g caster sugar. Soak 4 slices of white bread or brioche in the mixture then fry as above in 10g butter. Serve 2 slices per person.

A veritable paragon of student cooking, the cheese and ham toastie can be a gourmet's delight – melting cheese, toothsome ham and crisp toast make a lovely blend of textures. And it's not rocket science to produce. This recipe proves there is nothing wrong with simple food as long as you are using good ingredients, says John. Swiss gruyère is an excellent cheese to have on hand if cooking because it melts beautifully and has a strong, nutty flavour.

gruyère cheese & ham toasties

Serves 2
4 slices bread
4 slices gruyère cheese
4 slices ham
50g butter
30ml vegetable oil

Lay the bread on a work surface and cover each with a slice of cheese. On top of two, lay the ham.

Sandwich the other two pieces of bread on top so that you have two sandwiches comprising bread, cheese, ham, cheese, bread in that order. Press together lightly. Butter the outsides of the bread.

Heat the vegetable oil in a large frying pan. Carefully slide in the toasties and cook steadily until golden brown underneath. Use a spatula to help you turn the toasties over and cook the other sides.

Briefly drain the toasties on kitchen paper to remove any excess oil, and eat while still hot.

Too often forgotten, this classic British dish of toast with a layer of softened, browned savoury cheese on top makes a great breakfast, lunch or supper. John recommends serving it to guests with a lovely white wine, or a really good beer. Caerphilly, Wales's traditional cheese, has a moist, crumbly texture and salty taste that make it quite different from cheddar. It is available from supermarkets as well as retailers of artisan-produced cheese.

welsh rarebit

Serves 4

250ml milk

50g butter

20g plain flour

200g caerphilly cheese, grated

2 egg yolks

1 tsp English mustard

salt

cayenne pepper

Worcestershire sauce

4 slices bread

Heat the milk in a small saucepan until warm through but not bubbling.

In a separate, heavy-based saucepan, melt the butter. Add the flour, mix well and cook for a few minutes over a low heat.

Slowly stir in the warm milk, little by little, beating the sauce well after each addition to avoid lumps.

Remove the pan from the heat and stir in the grated cheese. Add the egg yolks, mustard, salt (if needed), plus the cayenne pepper and Worcestershire sauce to taste.

Toast the bread on both sides under a medium grill. Spoon the cheese sauce mixture over the toast, then return to the grill and brown the top.

Decent ready-made pastry is widely available in supermarkets, but making your own lets you choose the quality of ingredients used. It also allows you to add tasty flavourings such as the cheese and poppy seeds featured here.

cheese & poppy seed pastry

✳ ✳

Makes 2 x 23cm flan cases -
375g plain flour, plus extra
   for dusting
15g salt
225g unsalted butter, cubed,
   plus extra for greasing
1 egg
2 tsp poppy seeds
50g cheddar cheese, grated

In a jug or small bowl, beat the egg together with 4 tablespoons of cold water and the poppy seeds. Pour them into the flour mixture and add the grated cheese.

Sieve the flour and salt into a mixing bowl. Tip the cubed butter into the bowl and gradually rub it and the flour between your thumb and fingers until the mixture resembles fine breadcrumbs.

Slowly bring the ingredients together to form a ball, being careful not to overwork the pastry.

Knead the pastry lightly on the work surface, then wrap it in cling film and refrigerate for 30 minutes. Meanwhile, take one or two flan tins 23cm in diameter and 3cm deep and grease with butter.

Pick up the pastry by rolling it on to the rolling pin, then hold it over the flan tin and unroll the pastry so that it lays over the tin. Pick the edge of the pastry up with one hand and use the other hand to ease the pastry into the corners of the tin, working all the way around.

Preheat the oven to 200°C/gas 5. Cut a circle of greaseproof paper large enough to cover the base and sides of the flan. Sit it in the pastry case and pour in baking beans (or raw rice) to keep the paper weighed down.

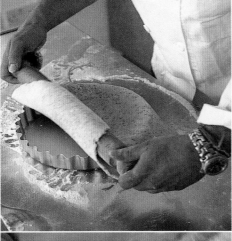

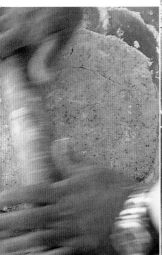

Cut the chilled pastry in half and roll one piece out on a clean work surface dusted with flour. The circle of pastry needs to be 2-3mm thin and slightly larger than the flan ring.

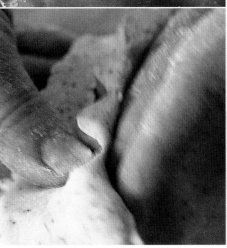

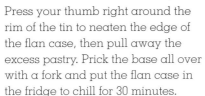

Press your thumb right around the rim of the tin to neaten the edge of the flan case, then pull away the excess pastry. Prick the base all over with a fork and put the flan case in the fridge to chill for 30 minutes.

Bake the pastry case for 12-15 minutes, then open the oven door, slide out the tart tin and lift out the beans and paper. Continue cooking for another 3-5 minutes, or until the pastry is golden brown and crisp.

pastry masterfile

From homely cheese biscuits to classy cocktail snacks, comforting pies to elegant fruit galettes, the basic skills for making shortcrust pastry will prove useful for many years, and many different occasions. Here are some quick ideas to get your new career as a pastry chef underway.

Make once, use twice

The pastry recipe on page 30 makes enough for two large tart cases, but you don't have to use it all at once. Uncooked pastry can be wrapped in cling film and stored in the fridge for several days before baking, or frozen for a week. You could even bake both tart cases and freeze one for up to three months.

Snappy snacks

For anchovy snaps, a sophisticated cocktail nibble, roll the pastry out very thinly to a square about 20cm and cut it in half. Pat dry some anchovies packed in oil. Lay one beneath the other across the width of one piece of pastry. Brush the other lightly with water and lay it damp-side down over the anchovies, pressing down firmly between the anchovies. Brush with melted butter, then cut down the length of the pastry, through the anchovies, to give equal strips. Bake for about 8 minutes, or until golden, at 190°C/gas 5.

Biscuits and straws

Cheese and poppy seed pastry makes excellent cheese biscuits. Feel free to use other firm, tasty varieties, such as comté and gruyère. Roll out the pastry and cut it into discs (or whatever shape you like). Put them on a baking sheet. Brush with melted butter, sprinkle generously with grated cheese, dust with cayenne pepper, then bake for 20 minutes at 180°C/gas 4. Another option is to cut the pastry into long strips about 1cm wide and twist them to make cheese straws. Lay them on a baking sheet, brush with melted butter and sprinkle with good quality, finely grated parmesan. They're very nice served before dinner with a glass of sherry or champagne.

For plain shortcrust pastry

To make plain shortcrust for savoury dishes, follow the steps on page 30, leaving out the cheese and poppy seeds. You could also make the pastry in a food processor, in which case use the paddle attachment and slowly add the butter piece by piece.

Sweet shortcrust pastry

This is made using the same techniques as shown on page 30, but with the addition of a little sugar and no savoury flavourings.

Here is the perfect pastry recipe to use for the lemon and passion fruit flan on page 231:

Rub together 70g icing sugar, 90g diced butter and 210g plain flour in a mixing bowl. Add a beaten egg (no water this time) and mix until the pastry starts to come together, being careful not to overwork it.

Shape the pastry into a ball and wrap in cling film before leaving it to rest in the fridge for a minimum of 20 minutes.

The most decadent pastry

Rich sweet pastry is made in a similar way but with different proportions of ingredients to give a really decadent flavour.

To make it, put 500g plain flour and a pinch of salt in a mixing bowl and rub in 300g of unsalted butter until the mixture is the consistency of breadcrumbs. Stir in 150g caster sugar.

Beat 3 eggs until smooth, then stir into the flour mixture adding just a little at a time. Be careful not to overwork the pastry by stirring too much at this point.

Roll into a ball, wrap in cling film and chill until firm. Then you can use it for recipes such as the vanilla custard tart and plum and almond tart on pages 228 and 232 respectively.

Tartlets and canapé cases

Don't forget you're not restricted to large tart cases when making pastry. A recipe that produces two large tarts could be used to make 10 individual tart cases 8-10cm in diameter. If planning a party, the same quantity will give 60 mini tartlets to serve as canapés.

Choc-chip cookies

A great way to get the kids interested in cooking: you can make chocolate chip cookies with any excess rich sweet pastry by rolling the pastry 1-1.5cm thick and stamping it into shapes with a biscuit cutter. Lay them on a baking sheet and press a few chocolate chips into each. Bake for 8-12 minutes at 180°C/gas 4.

More biscuit ideas

For sweet biscuits good to serve alongside creamy desserts such as fools and possets, or with fruit compotes, mould the rich sweet pastry into a fat sausage about 7.5cm wide, wrap it in cling film and leave in the fridge until really firm. Use a knife to slice the cold pastry into discs and lay them out on a baking sheet. Cook at 180°C/gas 4 for 8-12 minutes until they are just golden, then remove the biscuits from the oven and, while they are still warm, sprinkle them very generously with caster sugar (a shaker is best for this).

Perfect for a weekend lunch served with salad, or as a generous starter, John's moreish flan has a luscious creamy filling rich with tangy chunks of bacon and a crunchy pastry base studded with poppy seeds.

cheese, onion & bacon flan

Serves 8

1 baked cheese and poppy seed pastry shell (page 30)

For the filling

1 medium onion, sliced

20g butter

125g bacon

2 eggs

150ml milk

150ml whipping cream or crème fraîche

salt, pepper and finely grated nutmeg

1 tbsp chopped parsley

100g gruyère or cheddar cheese, grated

To make the filling, put a frying pan over a medium heat, add the sliced onion and butter and cook gently, stirring occasionally, until the onion is soft.

Grill the bacon for a few minutes on each side, then allow it to cool before cutting it into strips.

Whisk the egg, milk and cream together and add some salt, pepper and nutmeg to taste. Stir in the parsley.

Put the softened onion in the base of the pastry case. Top with the grated cheese and bacon, then pour in the egg mixture.

Carefully slide the flan into the oven so that the filling doesn't spill out and bake for 20-25 minutes or until the eggs are set and the surface of the flan is golden brown.

Tip

A metal fluted tin with a removable base is the best choice for flans. Metal conducts heat better than ovenproof china or glass, and the loose base will make the flan easy to lift out after baking.

The goat cheese you use here should be very fresh and soft, so that it will absorb readily into the béchamel sauce, helping the soufflé rise perfectly. John recommends a raw milk cheese no more than three or four weeks old.

twice-baked goat cheese soufflés

Makes 10

For the béchamel sauce
1 clove
1 small onion, peeled but left whole
455ml milk
1/4 bay leaf
1 thyme sprig
pinch of grated nutmeg
55g butter, plus a few dots extra
55g plain flour, sieved

For the soufflés
cold unsalted butter, for greasing
60g ground hazelnuts
320ml béchamel sauce (above)
9 eggs
1/2 tsp salt
pinch of cayenne pepper
pinch of grated nutmeg
*180g fresh goat's cheese such as
  crottin de chavignol*

Tip
*Be careful when folding
the last of the egg whites
into the soufflé base. It is
important not to overdo it
because the idea is to keep
as much air in the mixture
as possible.*

To make the béchamel sauce, stick the clove in the onion and place in a pan with the milk, bay leaf, thyme and nutmeg. Bring to a simmer.

Meanwhile, in another pan, melt the butter over a moderate heat. Blend in the flour and cook for a few minutes until the mixture (called a roux) begins to take on a little colour.

Gradually add the milk through a conical sieve (this will catch the flavourings), stirring well after each addition to give a smooth sauce. Turn the heat to low and cook for about 30 minutes.

Pour the cooked sauce through the conical sieve into a bowl. To stop a skin from forming on the surface, place one or two small pieces of butter on the top of the sauce while it is still hot. Set aside to cool.

Grease 10 x 8cm ramekins evenly with butter. Sprinkle in a little of the ground nuts, rolling the dishes around so the insides are evenly covered. Tap out any excess, then place in the refrigerator so the butter and nuts set.

Preheat the oven to 190°C/gas 5. Put 320ml of cooled sauce in a large stainless steel mixing bowl. Carefully separate the eggs and add the yolks to the sauce. With a strong balloon whisk, beat until completely smooth. Add the salt and season with cayenne and grated nutmeg.

Chop the goats' cheese as finely as possible and, using a whisk, beat it into the sauce mixture – this is now your soufflé base.

In a separate large clean bowl, whisk the egg whites until they form stiff peaks, taking care not to over-whisk them. Add half the stiff egg whites to the soufflé base, using a balloon whisk to stir until fully incorporated.

Add the remaining whites but this time use a plastic spatula to fold them very gently into the mixture. Remove the soufflé tins from the refrigerator and fill them to the top with the egg mixture.

Place a shallow roasting tray (large enough to hold all the soufflés) on the stove top. Quarter-fill with cold water and heat until it begins to boil.

Carefully add the soufflés to the roasting tray, making sure that the water does not reach any higher than halfway up the sides of the soufflé tins (if the soufflé mixture comes in contact with water it will be ruined).

Put in the oven for 15 minutes. When done, take the tray out and remove the soufflés. Carefully turn them upside down on a tray and remove the ramekins. As the soufflés cool, they will begin to shrink, but fear not! Once cold, they may be stored in the refrigerator for up to 24 hours.

To serve, preheat the oven to 190°C/gas 5. Butter a baking sheet and lay the soufflés down the middle. Bake for 7 minutes, until they rise again and turn golden. Serve immediately.

soups & stocks

Once you have had a really good French onion soup, you will find you can no longer settle for the versions sold in so many brasseries, says Angela. The traditional recipe includes madeira, a fortified wine also useful for making stock-based sauces, and although the soup takes a little longer to make than most, it can be a meal in itself. The result should be meaty and hearty, so use big Spanish onions rather than sweeter shallots or red varieties.

french onion soup

Serves 4
3 tbsp vegetable oil
5 large onions, sliced
50g butter
1 bay leaf
3 thyme sprigs
salt and pepper
200ml madeira
200ml beef or chicken stock (page 48)
½ baguette
50g gruyère cheese, grated
100g parmesan cheese, grated

Heat the oil in a large saucepan or casserole. Add the onions and cook over a medium heat until they start to colour.

Add the butter, bay leaf and thyme, and season with some salt and pepper. Continue cooking, scraping the bottom of the pan where the onions are sticking.

Once the onions are fully cooked and browned, add the madeira and let it boil until it has all evaporated. Pour in the stock, bring to the boil and simmer gently for 20 minutes over a low heat.

Meanwhile, cut the baguette into slices and toast them under the grill.

Adjust the seasoning of the soup to taste, then pour it into heatproof serving bowls and place them on a baking tray.

Sprinkle each portion of soup with gruyère cheese. Layer the toasted baguette slices on top and cover it with the grated parmesan.

Put the tray of soups under the hot grill until the cheese has melted and is golden brown.

A great way to use overripe tomatoes in summer, this unusual soup is one to which you can really add your personal stamp, says Angela. Like it sharp? Add some extra sherry vinegar and Worcestershire sauce. For a smoother finish, stir in a dash of cream. Although it might seem that burnt tomatoes will make the soup bitter, they impart a delicious gentle smoky flavour.

smoked tomato *soup*

Serves 4

1kg overripe tomatoes

100g sun-dried tomatoes, drained if packed in oil

150ml olive oil

500ml tomato juice

3 garlic cloves, crushed

1 tsp rock salt

handful basil and chervil stalks

1 tbsp sherry vinegar

few drops Worcestershire sauce

salt and pepper

few drops Tabasco sauce

shredded basil leaves, to garnish

Tip
This soup is a great one for entertaining as it can be made well in advance and served cold, like a gazpacho. Savvy menu planning such as this makes cooking for guests easier and more relaxing.

In a large bowl, mix together the fresh tomatoes, sun-dried tomatoes, olive oil, tomato juice, garlic and salt. Cover and leave to marinate in the fridge overnight.

Next day, preheat the oven to 180°C/gas 4. Pour the tomato mixture into a baking tray and bake for 25 minutes, or until the tomatoes just start to burn.

Remove the tray from the oven and scatter the herbs over the tomatoes. Cover and leave to infuse at room temperature for 30 minutes.

Transfer the tomato mixture to a liquidizer and blitz until smooth (or leave a little texture in the soup if you prefer).

Adjust the flavour as desired with sherry vinegar and Worcestershire sauce. Season to taste, then add a dash of Tabasco sauce for extra kick. Serve topped with shredded basil.

Two enduringly popular homestyle soups are lifted to restaurant calibre with the addition of some clever garnishes. Try making double the quantity and freeze the leftovers for comforting autumn and winter lunches.

leek & potato soup *with horseradish cream*

Serves 4
30g butter
100g shallots, chopped
1 garlic clove, finely chopped
150g leeks, chopped
300g potatoes, peeled and diced
1 litre chicken stock (page 48)
1 bunch chives
salt and pepper
150ml cream

For the horseradish cream
1 tbsp finely grated horseradish
½ tbsp lemon juice
100ml double cream
tiny pinch sugar
salt

To make the horseradish cream, mix the horseradish and lemon juice together. Stir in the cream and season with sugar and salt. Store in a screw-topped jar in the fridge.

Melt the butter in a large, heavy-based saucepan. Add the shallots, garlic and leeks, and cook gently, stirring occasionally, for 5 minutes, without colouring. Add the potatoes and cook gently for 2 minutes.

Pour in the stock and bring the mixture to the boil. Skim the froth from the surface. Simmer for 20 minutes or until the potatoes are very tender.

Trim the bases of the chives and add the trimmings to the saucepan. Remove the pan from the heat. Use a stick blender to liquidise the soup, or purée it in an upright blender.

Pass the soup through a fine sieve into a clean saucepan and bring the soup back to the boil. Skim the froth from the surface once more. Season to taste, then add the cream. Chop the remaining chives.

Pass about 40ml of the horseradish cream through a sieve, then whip until it forms soft peaks. Return the leftovers to the fridge for another day.

Ladle the soup into serving bowls. Spoon 2 teaspoons of horseradish cream into each bowl and sprinkle generously with chives.

pumpkin soup *with sautéed ceps*

Serves 4
1 pumpkin or large butternut squash, peeled, deseeded and cut into cubes
50g butter
2 tbsp white wine
about 50g rind of parmesan cheese, plus more diced parmesan to serve
about 900ml chicken stock (page 48)
little double cream (optional)
salt and pepper
few drops of truffle oil (optional)
1-2 tbsp olive oil
handful fresh ceps or other wild mushrooms, sliced

In a large saucepan or casserole, sweat the pumpkin cubes in the butter over a low heat to prevent any colouring.

Deglaze the pan with the white wine, then cover and allow the pumpkin to cook for 8-10 minutes, or until softened.

Add the parmesan rind and stock, and bring to the boil. Reduce the heat and simmer for 15-20 minutes, or until the pumpkin is very soft.

Discard the parmesan rind. Transfer the mixture to a liquidizer or food processor and blend until smooth. Pass the soup through a fine sieve and correct the consistency with more stock or a touch of cream. Check the seasoning and if you like, add a touch of truffle oil. Reheat the soup.

Meanwhile, heat the olive oil in a frying pan and briefly sauté the mushrooms until cooked.

Ladle the pumpkin soup into bowls and garnish with the mushrooms and parmesan before serving.

If you can use milky, fresh ears of sweetcorn rather than tinned for this mild, sweet-tasting soup, so much the better. Traditional New England chowder is a good way of introducing children to flavours such as chilli and garlic, says Angela. This recipe is also a lovely way to begin a dinner party and can even be served chilled. To make a vegetarian version, simply leave out the pancetta and use vegetable stock.

sweetcorn chowder

Serves 4
1 large potato
salt and pepper
50g butter
1 large onion, diced
1 garlic clove, chopped
1 red chilli, deseeded and chopped
100g pancetta lardons
500g sweetcorn kernels
200ml chicken stock (page 48)
200ml double cream
5 spring onions
3 tbsp crème fraîche
10 cherry tomatoes, quartered
1 tbsp chopped parsley

Peel the potato and cut it into 1cm cubes. Place in a pan of cold salted water, bring to a boil and simmer until just tender. Drain and refresh in cold water. Set aside.

In a large saucepan, melt the butter over a medium heat. Add the onion, garlic and chilli, and cook gently until tender but not coloured.

Meanwhile, in a small frying pan, fry the lardons until golden brown.

Add the lardons to the onion mixture, then add the sweetcorn and sweat for a few minutes.

Season the onion mixture with salt and pepper, then add the stock, bring to the boil and simmer for 10 minutes.

Add the potatoes and double cream, and bring back to the boil.

When the liquid is thick enough to coat the back of a spoon, add the spring onions, crème fraîche and cherry tomatoes, and let them heat through.

Sprinkle with the chopped parsley before serving.

This is a recipe to enjoy when you live or stay by the coast, says Angela. The shellfish, fennel, tomatoes and spices are redolent of summer and, although the soup seems very luxurious, it is in fact a fashionably frugal way of using leftover lobster bodies and shells. If you only have a few, you could make a small quantity and keep reducing the liquid to a sauce consistency to serve with seafood and pasta. Crayfish and langoustine are classic variations.

lobster bisque

Serves 4

2kg lobster bodies or shells
2 tbsp olive oil
1 large onion
1 large carrot
1 celery stick
1 leek
1 fennel bulb
1 lemon grass stalk, chopped
½ tsp rock salt
4 black peppercorns, crushed
4 coriander seeds, crushed
6-8 fennel seeds
3 thyme sprigs
1 bay leaf
1 tbsp tomato paste
375ml brandy
1 litre fish or chicken stock (pages 50 and 48)
3 plum tomatoes, chopped
200ml double cream

Preheat the oven to 160°C/gas 2. Chop the lobster bodies into similar-sized pieces. Spread them out on a baking tray, drizzle with half the olive oil and cook until they turn bright red, about 5-8 minutes.

Cut all the vegetables into dice of the same size. In a large saucepan or casserole, heat the remaining olive oil. When hot, add the onion, carrot, celery, leek and fennel, and cook, stirring occasionally, until golden brown.

Add the lemon grass, rock salt, peppercorns, coriander and fennel seeds, thyme and bay, and stir well. Add the tomato paste followed by the lobster bodies and mix them all together.

Pour in the brandy to deglaze the pan and let it bubble until it has evaporated. Cover with the stock and add the tomatoes. Bring to a simmer and cook for 30 minutes.

Pass the soup through a fine sieve into a clean saucepan, pressing down on the solids to extract all the juices.

Bring the soup back to the boil and taste. If necessary, boil it longer to reduce and concentrate the flavours.

Remove the pan from the heat. Add the cream and season to taste before serving.

Well-made stocks are the thing that sets fine restaurant kitchens apart from poor ones and they can transform your cooking, too. The French word for stock is *fond* or foundation, which reflects their importance in good cooking, yet a light, versatile chicken stock such as this one is easy to make at home. Stock cubes are full of salt and additives, John warns, and are unsuitable for making sauces as the more you reduce them the saltier the sauce becomes.

chicken stock

Makes about 2 litres

3 chicken carcasses

1 onion, peeled

½ carrot, peeled

1 leek

1 celery stick

2 garlic cloves, peeled

10 peppercorns

2 thyme sprigs

1 bay leaf

Tip

It is also possible to make stock using the leftover carcass from a roasted chicken, but remember: never use more water than you have bones. Add just enough to cover them. Too much water will make the stock grey and prevent it becoming gelatinous once chilled.

Wash the chicken bones. Break the carcass into several pieces and place in a tall pan or pot. Cover with cold water and bring to the boil. Skim well, using a ladle and taking the time to remove all the fat and sediment on the surface of the liquid.

Cut the onion and carrot into rough dice. Remove the dark green portion of the leek and discard. Wash the remainder under cold running water to remove all traces of dirt, then cut into short cylinders. Wash the celery stick and cut it into large dice.

Add all the vegetables and the garlic to the pan. Crush the peppercorns, and add them to the pan with the thyme and bay leaf. Make sure all the ingredients are pushed below the surface of the stock.

Bring back to the boil. Skim again and leave to simmer for 3 hours, skimming whenever necessary.

Strain the stock, discarding the solids, and allow it to cool. The stock can be stored in a covered container in the refrigerator for up to 4 days, or frozen in plastic lidded containers for up to 3 months.

Turbot and brill are particularly good for fish stock as their bones are very gelatinous; sea bream is excellent too, as its head has a lot of flavour. But the essential ingredient, says Angela, is patience – especially when skimming.

fish *stock*

Makes about 2 litres
3 tbsp olive oil
1 large onion, cut into chunks
1 leek, white part only, cut into
   chunks
1 celery stick, cut into chunks
1 whole garlic bulb, halved
1 fennel bulb, cut into chunks
5kg clean fish bones
2-3 white peppercorns,
   crushed
½ tsp rock salt
2-3 coriander seeds, crushed
2-3 fennel seeds, crushed
750ml white wine
handful parsley and chervil
   stalks

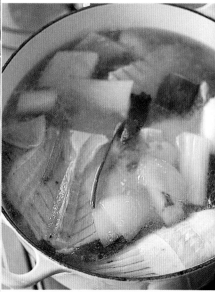

In a large saucepan, heat the olive oil and sweat all the vegetables, including the garlic and herbs, so that they are soft but not browned.

Add the peppercorns, rock salt, coriander seeds and fennel seeds. Deglaze the pan with the wine, then bring to the boil and reduce by half.

Lay the fish bones in the pan and pour in just enough cold tap water to cover (adding a few ice cubes at this point, too, will help produce a clearer stock).

Bring the pot to the boil, then use a ladle to skim all the froth that has collected on the surface of the liquid. Lower the heat so that the stock is simmering very gently.

Continue simmering for about 25 minutes (no more or the fish bones break down and impart a bitterness), skimming as necessary. Push the froth to the side of the pan by making circular motions with the ladle. Then run the ladle around the edge to remove the last of the froth.

Pass the stock through a fine sieve to strain it and, once it is cool, store in lidded plastic containers in the fridge for up to 4 days, or in the freezer for up to 3 months, remembering to label the containers with the date of freezing.

3 salads & dressings

Two side salads everyone needs to know how to make, and the good news is they are very easy. They needn't get boring: vary your choice of leaves and don't be afraid to be adventurous with vinegars, Angela advises.

tomato & basil *salad*

Serves 4
4-6 plum tomatoes
1 large punnet cherry tomatoes
small bunch of basil
2 tsp white wine vinegar
50ml olive oil
salt and pepper

Cut the plum tomatoes into wedges and put them in a salad bowl. Halve the cherry tomatoes or leave whole as desired, and add them to the bowl.

Pick the basil leaves from the stalks and, if large, tear them into small pieces. Sprinkle over the tomatoes.

Make a vinaigrette by mixing the vinegar and olive oil together in a small dish.

Season the tomatoes and herbs with salt and pepper.

Pour the vinaigrette over the tomatoes, mix and set aside to marinate for a few minutes before serving. Do not chill the salad: the tomatoes should be at room temperature.

classic leaf *salad*

Serves 4
400g mixed salad leaves
small handful mixed soft herbs, such as basil, chervil, dill and flat-leaf parsley
2 tsp white wine vinegar
50ml olive oil
salt and pepper

Wash the salad leaves in cold water and dry them gently in a salad spinner. Tear them into large bite-sized pieces with your hands. Check whether the herbs are dirty (especially the parsley) and if necessary wash and dry them too, in the same way.

Mix the salad leaves and herbs together in a large bowl.

Make a vinaigrette by mixing together the vinegar and olive oil in a small dish.

Season the leaves with salt and pepper, then pour the dressing over and toss using your hands to turn the leaves gently. Serve the salad as soon as the leaves are dressed.

A classic rustic dish from the Alsace region of France, this warm, hearty salad marries crunchy croutons with smoky bacon and the tang of cheese for a delicious result. With protein, carbohydrate and vegetables, this salad makes a complete meal, and a big bowl is just right for lunch, says John.

bacon & cheese salad *with creamed mustard vinaigrette*

Serves 4
olive oil
220g smoked bacon lardons
4 little gem lettuces
220g emmental cheese, cut into small
  slices

For the vinaigrette
1 tsp dijon mustard
splash of white wine vinegar
salt and pepper
pinch of sugar
55ml olive oil
dash of double cream
½ banana shallot, finely chopped
few chives, finely chopped

For the croutons
½ ficelle baguette
olive oil
1 garlic clove, peeled

Heat a little oil in a non-stick frying pan and fry the bacon lardons for a few minutes, or until golden. Remove from the heat and set aside.

To make the vinaigrette, combine the mustard, vinegar, seasoning and sugar in a bowl and whisk together.

Gradually whisk in the cream and just enough olive oil to emulsify the dressing. Stir in the shallot and chives, and adjust the seasoning to taste.

Pull off the outer leaves of the little gem and cut each one in half lengthways, then again crossways. Arrange on serving plates.

To make the croutons, cut the baguette at an angle into thin slices and drizzle them with a little olive oil.

Heat a large non-stick frying pan and, when hot, toast the bread slices on each side until golden brown and crisp. Remove the croutons from the heat and let them cool before rubbing each piece with the garlic to flavour them.

Place the croutons around the salad leaves. Scatter the bacon and cheese on top. Drizzle with the vinaigrette and serve.

Variation The creamed mustard vinaigrette is delicious in a potato salad with French saucisson, or served as a sauce alongside pieces of roasted cod.

The asparagus season only lasts a couple of months so make the most of it while you can, says Angela. This salad makes a great main course when served with a poached hen's egg, or trendy fried duck's egg or quails' eggs.

asparagus salad *with parma ham*

Serves 4

25ml white wine vinegar

150ml olive oil, plus more for the griddle pan

salt and pepper

30-40 asparagus spears, depending on their size

8 slices parma ham

parmesan cheese shavings

Tip
To make shavings of parmesan cheese, hold the wedge of cheese in your hand and run a vegetable peeler along the side.

Whisk the vinegar, olive oil and a pinch of salt together in a bowl to make a dressing and put to one side.

Heat a griddle pan and, when hot, drizzle it with a little oil. Remove the ends of the asparagus. Lay the spears on the griddle and cook lightly for 2-2½ minutes, or less if the spears are particularly thin. Do not let the spears get too dark on the griddle – they should still be green so that the flavour of the asparagus comes through.

Transfer the asparagus to a plate, season it with salt and pepper and pour a little of the dressing over. Cover the plate with cling film and allow the asparagus to finish cooking in the steam for a few minutes.

Place the asparagus on serving plates. Arrange the parma ham on the side and scatter with the parmesan shavings. Season with salt and freshly milled pepper, then drizzle with a little of the dressing and serve.

Here John combines the peppery bite of verdant watercress with the creamy acidity of young cheese, the sweetness of pear and the nutty crunch of a walnut and breadcrumb crust. The result is a plate of delicious and highly satisfying contrasts in taste and texture, making a rich starter or satisfying lunch or supper dish. As usual, he recommends buying artisan-made goat cheese made using unpasteurised milk.

pear, watercress & goat cheese salad

Serves 4

1 tbsp flour

1 egg

100g breadcrumbs

100g ground walnuts

4 x 100g soft goat cheese rounds

vegetable oil or olive oil, for frying

2 small pears

salt, pepper and sugar

50g watercress

about 4 tsp walnut vinaigrette
  (page 69)

Tip
Whenever you are coating an ingredient with egg and breadcrumbs, remember that it must first be dusted completely in flour. This ensures that the egg can cling to the food, and the breadcrumbs will consequently stick to it.

Put the flour in a dish or on a plate. Beat the egg in a bowl. Combine the breadcrumbs and walnuts in a separate dish, stirring to mix them evenly.

Take a portion each cheese and dust it in the flour so that it is evenly coated. Dip it in the beaten egg, turning so that the whole piece is covered with egg. Then place it in breadcrumbs, turning and patting the crumbs all over the cheese so that they form a crust. Repeat with the remaining cheese.

Warm a skillet or frying pan with a little oil. Add the cheese and cook steadily over a medium heat. When brown underneath, turn using a palette knife and cook on the other side.

Meanwhile, peel each pear, cut it into quarters and remove the core. Cut each quarter in half again and season with salt, pepper and sugar.

Heat a second skillet or frying pan with a little oil and add the pears. Cook over a medium-high heat, turning to brown on both sides.

Remove the caramelised pears from the pan and divide among the serving plates. Arrange the watercress on the plates.

Remove the cooked cheese from the pan and drain on kitchen paper. Position the cheese on top of the pears. Sprinkle the walnut vinaigrette around the edge of the plates and serve.

Angela recommends this clean-tasting salad for a summer lunch menu. The sweet taste of the orange and hint of honey in the dressing contrast beautifully with the slightly bitter bite of chicory and watercress. It's surprisingly popular with kids too. You could add a little finely grated ginger and chopped chilli to the dressing if desired, to give it a bit of kick.

orange & chicory *salad*

Serves 8

30g butter

100g whole walnuts

2 oranges

4 baby yellow chicory

40g coriander sprigs

40g mint sprigs

400g watercress

200g beansprouts

2 tsp sesame seeds

For the dressing

250ml olive oil

50ml cider vinegar

1 tsp clear honey

1 garlic clove, crushed

salt and pepper

Heat the butter in a frying pan and, when it starts to bubble, add the walnuts. Cook for about 5 minutes, or until the walnuts are coloured, shaking the pan from time to time. Remove and drain on kitchen paper.

Peel or cut all the rind and white pith from the oranges. Separate the flesh into segments, cutting between the membranes and catching the juice in a bowl. Put to one side.

Cut the chicory lengthways into quarters and brush lightly with the reserved orange juice. Pick the leaves from the herb sprigs.

Whisk all the dressing ingredients together in a bowl.

In a large salad bowl, combine the walnuts, orange segments, chicory, watercress and beansprouts, and toss.

Pour on just enough of the dressing to coat the ingredients lightly and toss again, adding the herbs. Sprinkle with sesame seeds and serve.

Variation Cut 2 corn-fed chicken breasts in half horizontally so that they open out like a book. Place between 2 sheets of cling film and bat them out to an even thickness. Brush with olive oil and cook on a preheated griddle for a couple of minutes on each side. Cut the chicken into strips and serve with the salad.

Here John aims to improve on the classic Italian dish beef carpaccio by giving it a French slant. Unlike the original, which features very thinly sliced raw meat, in this version the beef is seared and cut a little thicker so that you can fully enjoy its flavour and texture. Tiny cubes of salty creamy roquefort, France's famous blue vein cheese made with sheep's milk, make a piquant contrast – but you could use British stilton if you prefer.

rare fillet of beef *with roquefort*

Serves 4

400g fillet of beef

10g peppercorns

10g juniper berries

10g coriander seeds

2 cloves

olive oil, for frying and sprinkling

1 lemon, halved

salt and pepper

240g roquefort cheese

50g mixed salad leaves

about 4 tsp tarragon vinaigrette (page 69)

Trim the beef fillet of all sinew and fat. Crush the peppercorns, juniper berries, coriander seeds and cloves together in a mortar until fine, or whiz in a spice grinder. Press the spice mixture into the beef fillet.

Heat a skillet or frying pan and add a little olive oil. When the oil is smoking hot, lower the fillet into the pan and cook over a high heat until brown all over, being careful not to burn the spices. Drain on kitchen paper and allow to cool completely.

Wrap the beef tightly in cling film, pulling it round and round the fillet. Place in the refrigerator or freezer to firm up a little.

Cut the beef into thin slices, then put the slices between sheets of cling film and tap gently with a meat mallet or rolling pin until very thin.

Lay the slices flat on serving plates. Sprinkle with lemon juice and season with freshly ground pepper and salt.

Cut the cheese into small dice and mix it with the salad leaves. Sprinkle with a little lemon juice and drizzle over the tarragon vinaigrette. Season with salt and pepper and toss lightly.

Divide the salad between the plates, placing the leaves in the centre, and serve.

Why make your own mayonnaise? Because then you know what's is in it, says John. Use good free-range eggs and good olive oil – though mix it with a neutral-tasting vegetable oil too so that the olive flavour is not overpowering.

making mayonnaise

2 egg yolks

1 tbsp dijon mustard

40ml white wine vinegar or
    tarragon vinegar

200ml olive oil

150ml vegetable oil

salt and freshly ground black
    pepper

pinch of sugar

2-3 drops lemon juice

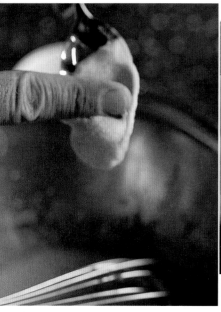

First make sure all your ingredients and equipment are at room temperature, then combine the eggs yolks, dijon mustard and vinegar in a basin.

Using a wire balloon whisk, mix them together for about a minute, until the mixture is thick and completely smooth. (Alternatively you can make mayonnaise in a food processor, following these same steps, but the result will not be as thick.)

Mix the olive oil and vegetable oil together in a jug and add them to the egg mixture in a slow, steady stream, whisking continuously as you do so.

If you find the mayonnaise becomes too thick as you are whisking in the oil, stop and add a teaspoon of warm water to thin it out, then continue adding oil. Stop whisking in the oil when you achieve the consistency you prefer.

Season the mayonnaise with a little salt, a pinch of sugar and a twist of freshly milled black pepper. Add a couple of drops of lemon juice to taste and mix well.

Use as needed and store any leftover mayonnaise, covered with cling film in the fridge, where it will last for 3-4 days.

dressing for success

What's the point of buying ready-made salad dressings when they are so easy to make yourself from fresh ingredients? With these ideas for mayonnaise and vinaigrettes, a great salad is always just a few steps away.

Use the blender

You can make your mayonnaise in a liquidizer or small food processor, but it is still essential to add the oil in a slow, steady stream so that the sauce emulsifies properly. If it seems to be thickening too quickly, stop the motor and add a teaspoon of warm water to thin the mixture before continuing with the oil.

Mustard, tarragon and other flavours

There are many quick and easy ways to add variety to homemade mayonnaise. Stir in a generous quantity of chopped fresh dill to serve with new potatoes and poached salmon, or sprinkle in some cayenne pepper to go with burgers and hotdogs. Mustard mayo is made simply by adding extra mustard (wholegrain if you like) to the basic recipe. If you want to make basil- or tarragon-flavoured mayonnaise, blanch the leaves first for a few seconds in boiling water, cool in an ice bath and squeeze dry before chopping and adding to the mayonnaise.

Other uses for mayonnaise

Use any leftover mayonnaise to make delicious egg sandwiches. Just chop some hard-boiled eggs, stir in a few spoonfuls of mayonnaise and plenty of freshly ground black pepper, and spread the mixture over the bread, topping it with fresh cress.

Another option is to make russian salad by stirring cooked diced carrot, potatoes and peas into the mayonnaise. Serve with other salads or flatbreads as part of a mezze table.

Alternatively, blend a small can of tuna with the mayonnaise, adding some chopped capers and anchovies. This sauce is traditionally served with thin slices of poached veal but is also delicious served with roast chicken.

Homemade tartare sauce

A classic served with grilled, crumbed or battered fish, this made by adding chopped fresh parsley, gherkins and capers to mayonnaise. Be sure to squeeze the capers dry before use, so they don't add too much briny flavour to the sauce.

Tarragon vinaigrette

Vinaigrettes are even easier to make than mayonnaise. They still need to be emulsified by whisking the oil into the vinegar base (or even shaking , if you combine them in a jar), but as there is no egg there is no risk of curdling.

This recipe for tarragon vinaigrette has a bold herby flavour that goes perfectly with the Grilled red mullet niçoise on page 110, and other light dishes of fish or chicken..

In a bowl, whisk 80ml white wine vinegar with a small pinch each of salt and pepper until the salt has dissolved. Steadily whisk in 250ml olive oil, then a drop or two of lemon juice to help lift the seasoning.

Smash a fresh peeled clove of garlic with the heel of a knife and place it in a clean storage jar or bottle. Add 10-15g carefully washed and dried sprigs of fresh tarragon.

Pour the vinaigrette into the jar and leave to infuse for at least 24 hours before using. The vinaigrette will last for up to 2 weeks in the fridge.

Making balsamic dressings

Balsamic vinegar has a rich, sweet flavour that needs to be used judiciously. To make balsamic dressing, whisk together 5 tablespoons olive oil and 1 tablespoon of the best balsamic vinegar you can afford, adding a little sea salt. That's it! This sweet-tasting dressing goes particularly well with the acidity of tomatoes and strong-tasting or bitter leaves like rocket or radicchio. You could also use it instead of a sauce to quickly dress a piece of grilled or roast lamb or fish.

Walnut vinaigrette

Whisk 50ml sherry vinegar together with a pinch each of salt, pepper and sugar until dissolved. Combine 100ml groundnut oil with 100ml walnut oil and whisk them into the vinegar mixture. Cut a small garlic clove in half and add it to the vinaigrette. Store in a clean jar or bottle in the fridge. To make hazelnut vinaigrette, simply replace the walnut oil with hazelnut oil – and remember to mix the nut oil half-and-half with a neutral tasting oil such as groundnut or vegetable oil, otherwise it will taste too strong.

Dress leaves, and vegetables too

Remember always to thoroughly dry salad leaves before tossing them with vinaigrette, and to add the dressing at the last minute before serving, otherwise the acid in the mixture will start to break down the leaves. The exception to this rule is when you are making a salad with cooked vegetables such as potatoes, leeks, cauliflower or green beans, in which case add the vinaigrette when the ingredients are still warm, so they can absorb the flavours.

poultry & game

4

Angela's unusual darkened twist on homely roast chicken is an aromatic option for dinner parties. The sweet and sour flavours of the glaze can be varied to suit your personal taste: add more garlic for a robust flavour, more cinnamon and mixed spice if you want it sweeter, or try a different type of mustard. Honey can be substitued for the maple syrup, too, but whichever you choose remember it will burn easily, so don't let it blacken too much.

roast chicken *with maple glaze*

Serves 4-6

1 free range chicken, about 1.5-2kg
salt and pepper
1 lemon, cut into wedges
1 garlic bulb, cut in half,
  cloves separated
handful of parsley stalks
115g butter

For the glaze
200ml maple syrup
2 garlic cloves, thinly sliced
¼ tsp ground cinnamon
¼ tsp mixed spice
3 tbsp wholegrain mustard
1 lemon
50ml sherry vinegar

Preheat the oven to 180°C/gas 4. Sit the chicken on a large sheet of foil in a roasting tray and season with salt and pepper.

Add the lemon, garlic and parsley stalks, and dot the chicken with the butter. Fold up the sides of the foil. Pour a glass of water over the chicken, seal the foil and place in the oven for 45 minutes.

Carefully open the foil package to expose the skin of the bird and continue roasting for another 15-20 minutes.

Meanwhile, make the glaze. Bring the maple syrup to the boil in a pan. Add the garlic, cinnamon and mixed spice. Then add the mustard, mixing well, and season with salt and pepper.

Finely grate the zest of the lemon and add it to the glaze. Squeeze the juice from half of the lemon and add it to the saucepan along with the sherry vinegar.

When the skin of the chicken is coloured and the flesh is almost cooked, baste the skin with the maple glaze and return it to the oven. Cook for a final 10 minutes, allowing the glaze to turn quite dark. The chicken is done when you pierce the thickest part of the thigh with a skewer and the juices that run out are clear, not pink or bloody.

Leave to rest for 10 minutes before carving.

An extravagant and surprisingly easy dish to serve when you have friends over, these little roast chickens are filled with a mixture of pork sausage-meat and sweet, succulent dates. Angela favours baby chickens over poussin, though you could use them instead. Be sure to buy free-range, corn-fed varieties. You could also use this basic recipe for a fully grown bird, in which case you will need to extend the cooking time by at least 30 minutes.

stuffed baby chickens

Serves 6
50g butter
1 large onion, chopped
salt and pepper
4 pork sausages
8 semi-dried dates such as medjool, finely diced
2 tbsp chopped parsley
3 baby chickens, each about 500-600g

Preheat the oven to 180°C/gas 4.

In a small frying pan, melt the butter and fry the onion in it until coloured. Season with some salt and pepper.

Cut the sausages lengthways then peel off and discard the skins.

Put the sausagemeat in a bowl and add the cooked onion, dates and parsley. Season with salt and pepper and mix well.

Stuff the cavity of each baby chicken with one-third of the sausage mixture. Put the stuffed chickens on a roasting tray and season well.

Roast the birds for 20-30 minutes, or until the skins are golden brown and the stuffing is totally cooked. To test, press a skewer into the birds, then remove and place it against your hand: it should be hot and any juices that run should be clear and not pink.

Let the birds rest in a warm place for about 10 minutes before serving.

While John is best known for his take on French cuisine, he has a passion for the food of the East, where he grew up. Even in Thailand, many people use ready-made curry pastes bought at the market for cooking, and they are readily available at Western supermarkets, but here John wanted to show how quick and easy it is to cook a delicious curry from scratch. Plus you have the confidence of knowing that all the ingredients are entirely natural.

Thai green curry *with jasmine rice*

Serves 2

8 spring onions

2 chicken breasts, skin removed

75g jasmine rice

2 tbsp vegetable oil

2 large green chillies, deseeded and finely chopped

2 garlic cloves, crushed

juice and grated zest of 3 large limes

1 tsp ground kaffir lime

1 tsp ground lemon grass

1 tbsp Thai fish sauce (nam pla)

1 x 400ml can coconut milk

25g coriander

Put a large pan of water on the stove and bring to the boil.

Meanwhile, take six of the spring onions, slice them across thickly at an angle and set aside. Cut the remaining two spring onions lengthways into very thin strips and set them aside separately to use as a garnish.

Cut the chicken breasts into bite-sized pieces.

Rain the rice into the pan of boiling water and cook for 10 minutes or until tender.

In a wok, heat the oil over a high heat and, when hot, add the sliced spring onions, chillies and garlic. Stir continuously with a wooden spoon so that the ingredients do not burn. Cook for 1 minute.

Add the chicken and keep it moving around the wok so that it does not stick. Cook for 4 minutes, or until the chicken is sealed all over.

Reduce the heat slightly and add the lime zest, kaffir lime and lemon grass. Stir well so that the chicken absorbs all the favours.

Add the fish sauce, followed by the coconut milk and stir well. Pour in the lime juice, stir again, then reduce the heat and leave the curry to simmer for 10 minutes, stirring occasionally.

In the meantime, roughly chop the coriander leaves and discard the stalks. About 2 minutes before the end of cooking, add most of the coriander to the wok, keeping some back to sprinkle over at the end. Stir the curry to mix in the coriander.

Drain the rice in a colander or sieve and place it in a serving dish or individual bowls. Sprinkle the curry with the shredded spring onions and the remaining coriander, and serve immediately.

Stir-frying is a terrific technique to use for quick suppers and you need not be restricted to authentic Chinese flavour combinations, as Angela's contemporary version with balsamic vinegar and fresh tarragon shows.

stir-fried chicken *with asian greens*

Serves 2

2 tbsp groundnut oil

2 skinless free-range chicken breast
   fillets, cut into strips

1 garlic clove, crushed

1 tsp grated ginger

1 star anise

½ tsp finely chopped red chilli

handful of mangetout

2 pak choi, stems separated

4 spring onions, sliced at an angle

100g mixed wild mushrooms,
   trimmed and cut into even-sized
   pieces

4 tbsp soy sauce

2 tbsp balsamic vinegar

handful of flat-leaf parsley sprigs

1 tbsp chopped tarragon

1 tbsp chopped chives

Tip
Stir-fries are a great way to use up small amounts of food in the fridge – just add some rice and you have a complete meal. Be organised and have all the ingredients ready before you heat the pan, as they will cook very quickly.

In a large frying pan or wok, heat the groundnut oil over a medium-high heat.

Add the chicken and cook, lightly tossing, until it is almost done.

Add the garlic, ginger, star anise and chilli, and continue to cook for 30 seconds.

Add the mangetout, pak choi, spring onions and mushrooms, and stir-fry until they are all lightly cooked.

Finish with the soy sauce, balsamic vinegar and fresh herbs. Stir together briefly and serve immediately.

Here John reconsiders a classic French dish translated as 'chicken in a pot'. The traditional version, in which a whole stuffed bird is poached in a pot of stock, can make it look aneamic and unappetising, so in this quickly-cooked update the chicken breasts are first fried until the skin is crisp and brown.

poule au pot *with pork dumplings*

Serves 2

200ml chicken stock (page 48)

2 x 200g chicken breast fillets
  (skin on)

6 baby new potatoes

6 small shallots, peeled

6 baby carrots, peeled

1 stick celery, chopped

6 baby leeks

olive oil

For the dumplings

2 rashers smoked bacon, about 75g

1 garlic clove, chopped

1 tbsp chopped parsley

165g sausagemeat

To make the dumplings, blend the bacon, garlic and parsley together in a food processor or liquidizer.

Transfer to a mixing bowl, add the sausagemeat and mix well.

Roll the mixture into balls the size of a walnut. Place on a tray and keep in the refrigerator until required.

Preheat the oven to 200°C/gas 6. Bring the chicken stock to the boil in a wide, shallow saucepan or high-sided frying pan. Add the chicken breasts and simmer gently for 12 minutes. Lift the chicken from the stock and keep to one side.

Put the potatoes and shallots in the stock and cook for 7 minutes. Add the carrots and cook for another 5 minutes, then add the celery and leeks and cook for 5 minutes more. Remove all the vegetables from the stock and set aside in a warm place.

Put the dumplings in the stock and simmer for 5 minutes.

Meanwhile, in a heavy-based frying pan, heat a little olive oil. Place the chicken breasts in the pan skin-side down and cook over a moderate heat until the skin turns golden brown.

Transfer the chicken to an ovenproof dish and cook in the oven for 5 minutes, skin-side up.

To serve, spoon the vegetables and dumplings into the bottom of two serving bowls, then add some of the broth. Place the chicken on top, brush with a little more olive oil and serve immediately.

Using a chicken that has been cut into eight elegant portions means the chicken will cook more quickly than the usual four pieces, and it allows each diner to have a piece of both white and dark meat, says John.

chicken sauté *with wild mushrooms & white wine*

Serves 4

1.5kg corn-fed chicken

2 tbsp vegetable oil

salt

2 shallots, finely chopped

2 garlic cloves, finely chopped

50g fresh wild mushrooms, such as blewits, morels, ceps and pied de mouton, trimmed and chopped

100g button mushrooms, sliced

200ml dry white wine

500ml chicken stock (page 48)

100ml double cream

4 watercress sprigs

Tip
Don't even think about using a stock cube for this dish. The stock is reduced to form a sauce, which intensifies its flavour, so the artificial, salty taste of stock cubes would be a disappointment.

Pull the bird's legs away from the body and cut through the skin between the leg and body. Working on one side at a time, bend the legs outwards to break the joint, then cut through the flesh under the joint.

Hold the drumstick in one hand so that you can see the natural curve between it and the thigh. Cut firmly through the point where the two bones meet to give one thigh and one drumstick portion. Repeat.

Cut the bird along the breast bone to loosen the meat, then cut through completely with your knife or shears. Turn the bird over and cut the ribs and backbone away in one piece.

Cut the breast area, with wings still attached, in half to give two large breast portions. About three-quarters of the way along each breast, cut at an angle to give two wing portions with some breast attached. Finally, trim all the chicken pieces.

Heat the oil in a large heavy-based frying pan. Season the chicken pieces with salt and carefully lay them skin-side down in the pan. Cook over a medium heat until golden brown on both sides.

Reduce the heat and add the shallots, garlic and all the mushrooms. Cover and cook gently, turning the chicken often, for about 15 minutes.

Remove the lid and prick the legs with a skewer or fork to check whether they are done. If the juices that run out from the chicken are clear, it is cooked; if blood appears then more cooking is required.

When the chicken is cooked through, remove it from the pan and keep warm. Tip off any excess fat from the pan and return it to the heat. Pour in the white wine to deglaze the pan, scraping up any sediment with a wooden spoon. Bring to the boil and reduce the liquid by half.

Add the chicken stock and return the pan to the boil, skimming off any froth that forms on the surface of the sauce.

Strain the sauce through a fine sieve into a clean pan, reserving the mushrooms and shallots. Continue boiling to reduce and concentrate the flavour. Sprinkle the mushrooms and shallots over the chicken.

When the sauce has reduced by half, add the cream, bring back to the boil and cook for 2 minutes. Taste and season with a little salt.

To serve, place the chicken, mushrooms and shallots back in the sauce and bring to the boil to heat through. Divide the chicken among serving plates, giving each diner a piece of dark meat and a piece of white. Spoon over the sauce and mushrooms, and garnish with watercress.

Fresh morel mushrooms are without doubt very expensive, John admits, and their season – late summer – is limited, so this fine recipe uses the dried variety. Their flavour is pungent, so you don't need many. The accompanying leeks cut through the rich cream sauce and add a lovely texture.

chicken with morels, *leeks & new potatoes*

Serves 4

100g dried morels
4 chicken breast fillets or suprêmes
 (skin on)
salt
20ml oil
40g butter
2 shallots, finely chopped
20 jersey royal potatoes
20-30 baby leeks
2 tbsp white wine
300ml chicken stock (page 48)
100ml double cream
splash of marc de bourgogne
truffle oil, for drizzling

Tip
Morels have a hollow stem so there is always some sand in them. It is essential therefore to wash them thoroughly.

Soak the morels in a bowl of cold water for an hour to rehydrate them.

Remove any gristle from the chicken and season with a little salt.

Place a heavy-based skillet or frying pan over a moderate heat and add the oil. Lay the chicken breasts in the pan skin-side down and brown them evenly on each side. Reduce the heat to low and continue cooking, turning the chicken often.

In a separate pan, melt 30g of the butter. Add the shallots and cook slowly over a low heat, stirring occasionally.

Drain the morels through a fine sieve. Cut them in half and remove any sand or dirt. Squeeze the morels dry, add them to the shallots and cook for a few minutes more.

Bring a pan of salted water to the boil. Add the potatoes, return to the boil then adjust the heat to a simmer and cook for 10-15 minutes.

Boil another pan of lightly salted water and plunge in the leeks. Cook rapidly for 3-4 minutes, then drain in a colander and keep warm.

Add the wine to the pan of morels and allow it to boil until the liquid has reduced by two-thirds in volume.

When the potatoes are tender, drain them and keep warm.

Transfer the cooked chicken to a plate and keep warm. Drain off any fat from the skillet and pour in the contents of the pan of morels and the stock. Stir vigorously to scrape any caramelised cooking juices from the bottom of the pan and incorporate them in the sauce.

Bring to a boil and reduce rapidly by half. Add the cream and return to the boil. Whisk in the remaining butter. Add the marc de bourgogne and season with salt.

To serve, reheat the chicken breasts. Carve each one into four or five pieces and place them in the centre of serving plates. Drape the leeks over the chicken and drizzle with a little truffle oil. Spoon the potatoes around the plate and finish with the sauce, sharing out the morels equally.

France meets the Far East in this exciting fusion dish which offers all the spicy flavours of a good curry without a flood of sauce. The hot sweet glaze when combined with the crisp duck skin results in a toffee-like crust, under which is the succulently sweet duck meat. The key, says John, is to melt the layer of fat under the skin (a process known as rendering) and pour as much of it as possible out of the frying pan.

duck breast *with honey & spices*

Serves 4
2 tsp coriander seeds
1 tsp ground ginger
1 tsp ground mace
salt and freshly ground black pepper
4 duck breasts
8 tbsp runny honey
480g fine green beans
30g butter

Crush the coriander seeds using a pestle and mortar or grind in a spice grinder. Add the ginger, mace and a little black pepper and mix well.

Remove any sinew from the flesh side of the duck breast and score the skin with a sharp knife. Season with a little salt.

Place a dry skillet or frying pan over a moderate heat and, when hot, lay the duck breasts in the pan, skin-side down. Cook for 5 minutes to render the excess fat from the duck and make the skin crisp.

Carefully tip the fat out of the pan and turn the duck breasts over. Increase the heat and cook until the flesh is sealed.

Reduce the heat under the pan and sprinkle the spice mix generously over the skin of each duck breast.

Spoon the honey over the duck and continue cooking, basting often as the honey gets thicker and glazes the duck.

Meanwhile, bring a large saucepan of salted water to the boil. Add the beans and cook rapidly for 5 minutes, until the beans are squeaky.

Drain the beans, return them to a clean pan and add the butter. Toss to mix over a medium heat.

Turn the breasts over in the thick honey and, when cooked to the desired stage, remove them from the pan.

Slice the duck thinly across the grain and serve with the beans and a trickle of spiced honey around the plate.

Guinea fowl is an underrated, underused bird, says Angela. It has a slightly gamier flavour than chicken and, when handled unsympathetically, its lean flesh can be tough and dry. The mushrooms used here make a delicious juicy contrast. When cooking guinea fowl, don't be afraid to add some chicken or vegetable stock, or water, to the roasting tray to create steam and keep it moist. Another option is to lay sliced pancetta over the breasts.

guinea fowl *with wild mushrooms & sage*

Serves 4
1 guinea fowl
salt and pepper
2 whole heads garlic
500g mixed wild mushrooms
100g butter
6-8 sage leaves

Preheat the oven to 180°C/gas 4. Put the guinea fowl on a roasting tray and season well. Cut the heads of garlic in half and place them on the tray with the guinea fowl. Roast for 20-30 minutes, or until the skin of the bird is golden.

Meanwhile, wash and dry the mushrooms. Trim as necessary and cut into even-sized pieces. About 5 minutes before the guinea fowl is due to finish cooking, melt the butter in a frying pan and sauté the mushrooms for 5-6 minutes. Season well.

Remove the roasting tray from the oven and drain off all the excess fat.

Put the sautéed mushrooms in the roasting tray with the guinea fowl. Add the sage leaves and place in the oven so that the mushrooms can absorb the cooking juices from the bird. They will only need 1-2 minutes, so be careful not to overcook them.

Leave the guinea fowl to rest for about 10 minutes, then carve and serve with the mushrooms.

Most people just stick their turkey in the oven and leave it until it's totally ruined, says John. Here is a much better way of cooking it, one that allows you to prepare it calmly in advance, and ensures the legs are not overdone.

christmas turkey

✳ ✳

Serves 8

4kg turkey

*1 quantity of turkey stuffing
  (recipe overleaf)*

100g butter

salt and pepper

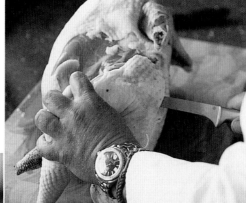

Remove the bones and sinew from both legs. Using a sharp knife, cut along the thigh and drumstick bone so that the bone is exposed. Slide the knife underneath the bone and cut along the underside to remove the entire bone.

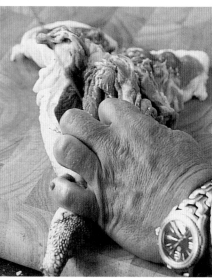

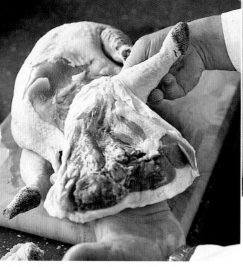

Remove the wings, wishbone and back from the turkey using a knife or a pair of poultry shears. Alternatively, ask the butcher to do this for you, but make sure he gives you the bones as they will be required for the sauce.

Pull the legs away from the body and cut along the natural line between the thigh and body to remove the leg joints in one piece. Put the turkey crown (both breasts on the bone) and the trimmed bones back in the refrigerator for use later.

At the drumstick end of the meat you will see sinew just under the flesh. Cut this out with a sharp knife and make sure that there is none remaining. Repeat this process for the second leg. You will be left with two rectangular pieces of meat.

With the stuffing in the middle of each piece of meat, pull the sides of the meat up and around so that they envelope the stuffing and resemble a large fat sausage.

Roll the sausage up inside the foil so that it is tightly wrapped. Squeeze both ends together so that the foil is sealed and the parcel resembles a Christmas cracker.

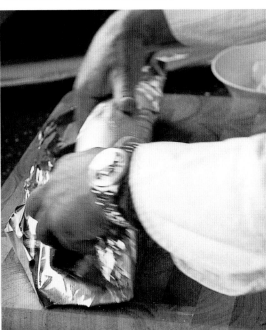

Once the meat is clean of all sinew and bone, season the flesh side with salt and pepper. Take the stuffing from the fridge and divide it equally between the two legs. Shape the stuffing into two cylinders that will fit down the centre of each of piece of leg meat.

Lay a large piece of foil out on the work surface and grease with a little butter. Lay the rolled-up leg across one end of the foil and sprinkle with some seasoning.

Repeat the process with the other turkey leg, then refrigerate the stuffed legs until required.

For the stuffing
4 onions, finely chopped
4 garlic cloves, finely chopped
25g butter
½ bunch sage, finely chopped
500g pork belly, minced
250g dried apricots, diced
1 egg, beaten
50g fresh breadcrumbs
salt and pepper

For the turkey crown
100g butter

For the sauce
1 carrot, chopped
1 onion, chopped
1 celery stick, chopped
½ leek, chopped
1-2 tbsp olive oil
4 garlic cloves, crushed
½ bunch thyme
1.2 litres chicken stock (page 48)

To make the turkey stuffing, sweat the onions and the garlic in the butter until soft but not coloured. Stir in the sage and set aside to cool.

When the onion mixture is cool place it in a bowl with the minced pork belly, apricots, egg and breadcrumbs and mix well. Season with salt and pepper, and refrigerate until needed.

To prepare the turkey crown, push your hand under the skin covering the breasts so that you make a pocket between the flesh and the skin. Take care not to tear or remove the skin.

Soften the butter by working it in a bowl with a wooden spoon. Season with salt and pepper. Use your hands to push the butter under the skin into the pocket you created. Make sure that you have an even covering of butter over both breasts, then set aside.

To make the sauce, preheat the oven to 200°C/gas 6. Chop the back and wings of the turkey into small pieces, put them in a roasting tin and roast until golden brown. Drain off any fat, then set the bones aside on a plate.

Add the carrot, onion, celery and leek to the roasting tin with a little olive oil and roast until golden brown. Drain any excess oil from the vegetables.

Combine the roasted vegetables and bones in a large saucepan with the garlic, thyme and chicken stock. Bring to the boil over a medium heat and skim off the froth that collects on the surface. Turn down to a gentle simmer and cook for about 1 hour.

Strain the stock through fine sieve, return to a clean saucepan and reduce to the required consistency. Keep warm until ready to serve.

To cook the turkey crown, preheat the oven to 200°C/gas 6. Place the turkey crown in a roasting tin and put it in the oven. Cook for approximately 45 minutes.

Turn the oven temperature down to 180°C/gas 4 and continue cooking the turkey crown for 1¼ hours to 1½ hours. If it starts to colour too much, cover it with foil.

Meanwhile, put the foil-wrapped turkey legs in a roasting tin and put them in the oven too. Cook for 20 minutes, then turn the parcels over and cook for another 20 minutes. Repeat this procedure twice more until the stuffed legs are cooked evenly all over.

When the crown is done, remove it from the oven and allow to rest for 20 to 30 minutes, before carving.

Once the legs are cooked, remove them from the oven and allow to cool slightly before removing the foil. Slice and serve immediately with the sauce and carved turkey breast.

Pearl barley is a traditional ingredient that shouldn't be forgotten, says John, as it is delicious and makes a beautifully textured alternative to potatoes.

roast pheasant *with pearl barley*

Serves 6

3 small hen pheasants, about 1.5kg each

6 rashers streaky bacon, rind removed

salt and pepper

90g pearl barley, washed

1 savoy cabbage, quartered and cored, the quarters cut across in half then shredded into short strips 1 cm thick

For the sauce

2 large onions, peeled

1 carrot, peeled

1 leek

1 celery stick

8 shallots, peeled

about 120g unsalted butter

olive oil (optional)

180ml dry white wine

1 litre chicken stock (page 48)

2 garlic cloves, peeled

1 thyme sprig

1 bay leaf

Tip
Before you cook the pheasants, make sure that your butcher or game dealer has removed the wishbones. This makes carving easier once the birds are cooked.

Preheat the oven to 200°C/gas 6. Start the sauce: chop one onion and the carrot, leek and celery into 2cm dice. Finely chop the second onion and the shallots. In a heavy pan, melt 30g butter and cook the finely chopped onion and shallots over very low heat, stirring often to prevent burning, for 30-45 minutes, until very soft. Ideally, cover with a sheet of buttered greaseproof paper so they steam. Purée in a liquidiser until smooth. Set side.

Season the birds and rub with a little butter. Lay two rashers of bacon over each breast. Place a large roasting pan over a moderate heat. Put the birds in it on their sides and brown each side. Transfer to the oven and roast for 15 minutes on each side and 10 minutes on their backs. About 5 minutes before the end, remove and reserve the bacon.

Meanwhile, bring a large pan of salted water to the boil and add the barley. Simmer for about 30 minutes, or until tender. Drain and let cool.

When the pheasants are done, remove from the oven and let rest for 10 minutes. Position a pheasant so it is facing you. Use a sharp knife to cut between the leg and the breast meat. With a fork, carefully pull the leg away from the carcass. Repeat on the other side. Holding the carcass still with a roasting fork, run the knife along the breastbone and remove the meat so that you have a whole breast fillet. Repeat on the other side, then with the other birds so you have six breast fillets and six legs. Keep warm.

Chop the remaining bones and skin, and put in the roasting pan. Brown slowly over a medium-low heat to avoid burning. Transfer to a saucepan. Brown the chopped onion, carrot, leek and celery in the roasting pan - you may need a little oil if there is no fat left. Transfer to the saucepan of bones.

Carefully tip any remaining fat out of the roasting pan and return it to the heat. Pour in the wine and, using a wooden spoon, carefully scrape up any sediment. Bring the wine to the boil and reduce by one-third. Add to the pan of bones. Add the stock, onion purée, garlic, thyme and bay leaf. Bring to the boil, skim off any froth and simmer for 20 minutes.

Boil the cabbage rapidly in a large pan of salted water for about 4 minutes. When tender, drain and spread on a tray to cool. Cut the reserved bacon into 1cm strips, sprinkle over the cabbage and dot a little butter on top.

Pass the pheasant stock through a fine sieve. Then pass it again through a sieve lined with muslin. Place in a clean pan and bring to the boil. Skim and boil rapidly to reduce by half.

Cover the carved pheasant with foil and reheat in the oven. Reheat the barley in a little of the stock. In a large pan, melt 30g butter and add the cabbage and bacon. Toss until warmed through, then season.

Divide the pheasant between serving plates. Spoon on the strained barley, arrange the cabbage in mounds and spoon over the sauce.

5 fish & shellfish

It is worth hunting down jars of authentic Spanish piquillo peppers for Angela's spicy crumb crust, as they have unique spicy flavour, but you could use ready-grilled or roasted red peppers instead. Romesco is a Spanish sauce made from pounded nuts and red peppers.

grilled prawns *with romesco crust*

Serves 4
100g piquillo peppers
salt and pepper
1 sprig rosemary, chopped
1 garlic clove, thinly sliced
50g blanched almonds
50g fresh breadcrumbs
20 large raw king prawns
3 tbsp olive oil

Tip
The quantity of crust here makes much more than you need for one dish but it's not worth making less. Instead keep the leftovers in the freezer and use on other occasions to add oomph to lamb or fish.

Spread the piquillo peppers out on a baking sheet. Season with salt and pepper, and sprinkle with the rosemary and garlic. Put them in the oven and leave them to dry overnight on the lowest temperature setting. They are done when darkened in colour and shrivelled.

Toast the almonds in the butter in a small pan over a low to moderate heat, stirring constantly to colour them evenly without burning.

Put the dried peppers in a food processor with the almonds and breadcrumbs and whiz to a powder.

Peel the prawns. Cut along their backs and use a toothpick or skewer to pull out the black intestinal threads.

Season the prawns. Heat a little olive oil in a frying pan and, when hot, sauté the prawns until they are just coloured on both sides.

Place in a serving platter and sprinkle with a little of the romesco crust before serving.

Everyone loves moules marinière, says John, and this recipe brings an Asian flavour to that French classic, with its inclusion of curry powder, saffron, fresh coriander and coconut milk. He recommends rope-grown mussels, which dangle in the water as they grow, rather than touching the bottom of the sea, ensuring that the mussels are not sandy.

curried mussels *with coconut*

Serves 4

1.5kg mussels
30g butter
2 shallots, finely chopped
1 garlic clove, finely chopped
1 tsp curry powder
1 celery stick, chopped
1 bay leaf
1 thyme sprig
150ml dry white wine
75ml coconut milk
pinch of saffron powder
1 tbsp chopped coriander

Wash the mussels, scraping the shells to remove any barnacles and pulling away the beards.

Melt the butter in a large saucepan and add the shallots, garlic, curry powder and celery. Cook gently for 5 minutes. Add the bay leaf and thyme.

Turn up the heat under the pan. Add the white wine and bring to the boil.

Tip in the mussels and stir to mix. Cover with a tight-fitting lid and cook for about 3 minutes or until the mussels open.

Shake the pan, and stir in the coconut milk, saffron and coriander. Remove the pan from the heat as soon as possible as you do not want the mussels to overcook or they will become rubbery.

Using a ladle, divide the mussels between four bowls then pour the broth over them and serve immediately.

Tip
Aim to buy mussels with closed shells. Sharply tap any that are open and if they close, they are safe to use; if they don't close you must throw them away.

Oily fish are very good for you and mackerel is one of the cheapest available, says Angela. It's also plentiful – something it is important to keep in mind in these days of dwindling fish stocks – and requires very little cooking to make a delicious supper. In fact, she even recommends trying thin slices raw in a marinade of oil and lemon. For an even easier meal, serve smoked mackerel, which needs no cooking, with this simple potato accompaniment.

mackerel *with crushed potatoes*

Serves 4

12-15 new potatoes
250ml olive oil
50ml white wine vinegar
salt and pepper
4 mackerel fillets
2 large basil leaves, chopped
1 tsp chopped chives

Put the potatoes in a saucepan of cold water and bring to the boil. Cook for about 15 minutes, or until tender.

Meanwhile make a vinaigrette by whisking half the olive oil, all the white wine vinegar and some salt and pepper together in a bowl, then leave it to one side.

To prepare the fish, run your hands lightly over the fillets checking for any bones. Use a sharp knife to score down the skin evenly along the length of the fish at 5mm intervals. Pinching the flesh makes it easier to score the skin. Set the fish aside.

When the potatoes are ready, drain them and peel while they are still warm (rubber gloves or a kitchen towel can help here).

Place the potatoes in a bowl and crush them with a fork. Stir in some of the vinaigrette and the chopped herbs.

Heat the remaining oil in a frying pan over a moderate heat. Place the mackerel in the pan skin-side down and cook gently until golden and the skin is crisp, 1-2 minutes. Turn and cook the other side in the same way.

Divide the crushed potatoes among serving plates. Add the fish fillets and drizzle with the remaining vinaigrette.

Although wild salmon is vastly superior to farmed, it is prohibitively priced because of its rarity. Fortunately, says Angela, much of the farmed salmon on sale today is better than it used to be, with high-quality organic varieties fairly easy to find in stores. She likes to serve salmon rare, or slightly undercooked at the centre. This mildly spiced recipe is also a good way of introducing children to the delights of eating fish.

pan-fried spiced salmon

Serves 4

1 garlic clove

sea salt

1 tsp grated ginger

pinch of curry powder

pinch of cumin

finely grated zest and juice of 2 limes
   or lemons

130ml olive oil

1 tbsp chopped coriander

4 salmon steaks

Using a mortar and pestle, crush together the garlic and a large pinch of salt. Add the ginger and continue to crush to a paste. Add the curry powder, cumin and lime zest.

Stir in 100ml of the olive oil, the lime juice and half the chopped coriander. Mix well.

Spread the spice mixture over the salmon steaks and leave them to marinate for 10 minutes.

Heat the remaining olive oil in a shallow frying pan over a moderate heat.

Cook the fish for about 3 minutes on each side, turning carefully.

Drain and serve sprinkled with the remaining coriander and accompanied by a small green salad.

Why not make a large batch of Angela's tasty fishcakes and store them in the freezer ready for producing quick meals? They make a great midweek supper, or even a glamorous lunch dish served with a dollop of mayonnaise.

fishcakes

Serves 4
500g salmon fillets
2 tbsp chopped parsley, stalks
    reserved for the poaching
100ml white wine
100g butter
salt and pepper
500g floury potatoes
juice of ½ lemon
pinch of cayenne pepper
5 tbsp mayonnaise (page 66)
plain flour, for dusting
breadcrumbs
1 egg, beaten
olive oil, for frying

Once cool, drain off the cooking liquid. the salmon into flakes and set aside. Meanwhile, peel the potatoes and cut them into even sized pieces. Put them in a saucepan of cold salted water, bring to a boil and cook until the potatoes are tender. Drain well.

Place the salmon in a wide pan. Add the parsley stalks, wine, butter and just enough water to cover the salmon. Season well. Place over a low heat and poach until the fish is just cooked. Leave it in the liquid until it cools down to room temperature.

Pass the potatoes through a ricer or mash them, and leave them to cool down.

When the potatoes are cool, stir in the chopped parsley, lemon juice, cayenne, mayonnaise and some salt and pepper, and mix well. Carefully fold in the flaked salmon and adjust the seasoning if necessary.

Put some flour and breadcrumbs on separate plates. Beat the egg in a dish. Working one at a time, dust each fishcake thoroughly in flour, then dip into the beaten egg and coat in the breadcrumbs.

Shape the mixture into ten cakes, roughly 100g each. Put them on a baking tray and chill for a couple of hours to help them set firm.

Heat a little olive oil in a frying pan over a medium heat. When the oil is hot, cook the fishcakes in batches, taking care not to overcrowd the pan, until golden on both sides. Check the inside of one to see whether it is hot through. If necessary, transfer the fishcakes to a baking tray and place in a 170°C/gas 3 oven until they are piping hot on the inside.

Fruit and fish go very well together, says Angela, but make sure you buy nice sweet varieties of grapefruit and orange for this dish so that the flavour is not too acidic. It makes a stylish main course for dinner parties. If you can only find halibut steaks, bake them with a little white wine and lemon juice in a moderate oven for 15-20 minutes, rather than frying them.

halibut *with grapefruit vinaigrette*

Serves 4

2 grapefruit

2 oranges

salt and pepper

4-6 mint leaves

50ml olive oil, plus extra for frying

2 tsp white wine vinegar

2 pak choi

4 x 130g portions halibut, skinned

1 tbsp chopped chervil

50g butter

100ml fish stock or chicken stock
    (pages 50 and 48 respectively)

Tip

Prepare the fruit and vinaigrette just before the fish gets cooked. You want to give the flavours time to infuse but if left for too long the segments will start to break down in dressing.

Peel and segment the grapefruit and oranges and season with salt. Finely shred the mint leaves.

Make a vinaigrette by whisking together the olive oil, vinegar and a pinch of salt in a bowl. Gently stir in the fruit segments and mint and set aside to infuse.

Cut the root off the pak choi, separate the stems, then wash, drain well and set aside to dry.

Season the halibut with salt and pepper. Heat a little olive oil in a frying pan and lay the fish in the pan skin-side down. Cook for about 3 minutes, until the underneath is a good golden colour.

Turn the fish over and sprinkle with the chervil. Add the butter to the pan and pour in the stock. Quickly cover the pan and cook for 3 minutes, or until the fish is just done, and the liquid in the pan is thick enough to coat the fish.

In a separate pan, heat some more olive oil and quickly sauté the pak choi over a moderate heat. Season well.

Place the pak choi in the centre of the serving plates. Spoon the grapefruit vinaigrette all around and, finally, lay the fish on top.

Fresh fennel is a crunchy vegetable that works terrifically well with fish but it should only be used when it is in season, during spring and summer, says Angela. The best comes from Italy (keep an eye out for wild fennel in specialist shops too) and don't forget that you can use the feathery fronds.

sea bream *with fennel & dill salad*

Serves 4
fillets from 2 whole sea bream
2 tbsp olive oil

For the salad
1 garlic clove, crushed
1 tsp coarse grain mustard
25ml white wine vinegar
150ml olive oil
salt and pepper
bunch of dill, chopped
*1 small fennel bulb, thinly sliced and
   soaked in iced water*

Trim the fillets and remove the pin bones by feeling along the flesh with your fingers and picking out the little bones with tweezers.

Score the fish skin with a sharp knife at 5mm intervals along its length.

Place the fillets in a tray skin-side up and leave in the fridge until ready to use.

To start the salad, combine the garlic, mustard and vinegar in a bowl and mix well. Whisk in the olive oil and season with salt and pepper.

Chop the dill and leave to one side until ready to use.

To cook the fish, heat a large frying pan with the olive oil. Lay the fish in the pan skin-side down and as it goes in, give the pan a little shake to help prevent sticking. Cook for 3 minutes, until the skin is crisp.

Meanwhile, drain the fennel and mix it with the chopped dill and vinaigrette. Arrange the salad on the serving plates.

You could use bream, sea bass or even inexpensive mackerel for this elegant dish. It's a salad, so the beans, potatoes and quails' eggs can be cooked well in advance, so that you need only grill the fish, dress the leaves and plate the food just before serving.

grilled fillet of red mullet niçoise

Serves 4

1 bunch basil

120ml olive oil

8 tiny new potatoes

32 green beans

4 quails' eggs

1 little gem lettuce

4 croutons

50g salad shoots (optional)

1 tbsp vinaigrette, such as tarragon vinaigrette (see page 69)

8 anchovy fillets

4 fillets red mullet

salt and pepper

lemon juice

For the tapenade

30g black olives, pitted

2 tsp ground almonds

1 tsp capers

6 anchovy fillets

1 garlic clove

1 tsp olive oil

Tip

For a restaurant-quality finish, make a crisp basil garnish. Stretch cling film over a plate like a drumskin. Brush lightly with olive oil, then press basil leaves into the oil. Cover with more cling film and microwave on high for 2 minutes. This technique works with sage leaves too.

To make the tapenade, combine the olives and ground almonds in a food processor, and blend to a fine paste. Add the capers, anchovy fillets and garlic, and blend again until smooth.

Transfer the paste to a bowl and mix in the olive oil. Add pepper to taste. Cover and chill until required.

Remove most of the stalk from the basil leaves and reserve four nice-looking leaves to use for garnish.

Bring a pan of lightly salted water to the boil and blanch the basil for 30 seconds. Drain then refresh in iced water. Squeeze the basil dry and put it in a liquidiser with 100ml olive oil. Purée for 3 minutes until completely smooth, then pass the basil oil through a fine sieve into a container and store in a cool place.

Bring the new potatoes to a boil in a small saucepan and cook for 8-10 minutes or until tender. Drain and set aside to cool.

In some more boiling water, cook the green beans for 2-3 minutes, then drain and refresh in iced water. Meanwhile, simmer the quails' eggs in a small pan of water for 2 minutes to hard-boil them, then drain and cool.

When they have cooled, peel and slice the new potatoes, then peel the quails' eggs and cut them in half.

Remove and discard any coarse outside leaves from the lettuce. Tear it into bite-sized pieces and mix with the salad shoots, if using.

Spoon four teaspoons of the tapenade on to the croutons and garnish with the reserved basil leaves.

Preheat the grill to the highest setting. In a heavy-based frying pan, heat the remaining 20ml of olive oil. Season the fish fillets with a little salt and place in the pan flesh-side down. Put under the hot grill and cook for 2 minutes, until the skin turns bright red.

Meanwhile, arrange the potato slices on serving plates and crisscross with the beans. Gently toss the salad with the vinaigrette and arrange on top of the potato. Decorate the plates with the halved quails' eggs and anchovy fillets.

Squeeze a little lemon juice on to each fish fillet and place them on top of the salads. Spoon around a little of the basil oil and serve.

A large bowl of this chunky summery stew makes an impressive main course for an informal dinner party. Angela encourages you to adapt the recipe to suit whatever fish is available – you could leave out the shellfish entirely if preferred – and try using rice or pearl barley instead of pasta.

fish stew

Serves 4

20 mussels

2 fillets sea bream, each about 350g

200g monkfish

8 large king prawns

4 ripe plum tomatoes

100ml olive oil, plus extra for drizzling

2 banana shallots, finely sliced

2 garlic cloves, crushed

200ml white wine

1 tsp finely chopped fresh red chilli

200g small pasta shapes, such as ditalini

1 tbsp chopped flat-leaf parsley

Wash the mussels, scrubbing the shells and pulling off the beards. Discard any open ones that don't close when tapped sharply. Cut each fillet of sea bream into three pieces and score the skin across at 5mm intervals. Cut the monkfish into bite-sized pieces. Remove the tail shells from the prawns but leave the heads intact. Set all the seafood aside.

Cut the tomatoes into halves or quarters and remove the seeds using a teaspoon. Cut the flesh into dice and set aside.

Heat two tablespoons of the olive oil in a large saucepan over a medium heat. Add half the shallot and all the garlic, and sauté for about 2 minutes, until they are soft but not coloured.

Raise the heat under the pan and, when hot, add the cleaned mussels. Pour in the wine then cover and cook for 4-5 minutes, or until the mussels are open. Discard any that remain closed.

Drain the cooking juices from the saucepan into a bowl and set aside. Pick the mussels from their shells, leaving about eight unshelled to use in the presentation. Set them all aside.

Heat a wide pan with two more tablespoons of the oil over a moderate heat, add the chilli and the rest of the chopped shallot, and lightly sauté.

Pour in the mussel stock and 250ml water and bring to the boil. Add the pasta and cook for 5 minutes.

In a separate frying pan over a moderate heat, sauté the monkfish, prawns and sea bream in the remaining oil, putting the largest pieces in first so they all cook in roughly the same time. Add them to the stew.

Add the diced tomatoes and cooked mussels and allow them to heat through gently, stirring lightly. Sprinkle with the parsley and finish with a generous drizzle of olive oil before serving.

This recipe from John uses a readily available flat fish, lemon sole, but the tangy salsa will work with many other varieties of fish, including plaice and brill, which are filleted in the same way.

fillets of sole *with avocado & lime salsa*

Serves 4

2 whole lemon sole, or 800g lemon
*   sole fillets, skin removed*
salt and pepper
flour, for dusting
40ml olive oil
juice of 1 lemon half
1 chervil sprig

For the salsa
4 plum tomatoes
2 avocados
1 small red onion
1 garlic clove
½ chilli
juice of 1 lime
3 tbsp olive oil
handful of coriander, chopped
chervil sprigs, for garnish (optional)

Tip
Wash your hands straight after chopping the chilli so that it does not irritate your skin.

Run a filleting knife along one side of the fish's backbone, down to the bones. Keeping the knife flat, run it underneath the fillet against the carcass to remove the fillet in one piece. Repeat on the other side, then turn the fish over and remove the last two fillets. Repeat with the second fish.

Lay each fillet skin-side down, tail end toward you. Make an incision just above the tail end. Grasp the end of the skin in one hand and, holding the knife parallel to the work surface, run it between the skin and flesh in a sawing motion to remove the skin. Repeat with the other fillets.

Put the fish on a tray or plate and season with salt. Dust with flour and tap off any excess.

To make the salsa, bring a pan of water to the boil. Cut a cross in the base of the tomatoes and put them in the boiling water for a minute or two. Drain, and peel the loose skins away from the tomato flesh.

Quarter the tomatoes and scoop out the seeds using a teaspoon. Cut the flesh into 1cm dice and place in a mixing bowl.

Peel the avocados. Halve them vertically and split them open to remove the stones. Cut into 1cm dice and add to the tomatoes. Peel and finely chop the onion and garlic and add them to the bowl.

Cut the chilli in half and carefully remove the seeds. Chop the flesh very finely and add it to the salsa. Add the lime juice, olive oil and coriander to the salsa, mix well and set aside.

Heat the oil in a large frying pan. Lay the fillets in the pan skin-side down and cook over high heat for 1½ minutes or until crisp and golden underneath. Turn the fish over, cook for 1 minute, then turn off the heat.

Arrange the fish on warm plates with the salsa. Sprinkle with lemon juice and decorate with chervil if you like before serving.

John insists on wild salmon when he cooks this dish, but suggests sea trout and brown trout as suitable alternatives. The sauce also works well with delicate white fish like sole and john dory. For the uninitiated, John likens sorrel to basil, but sorrel has a lemony acidity that cuts through the rich fish.

salmon *with sorrel butter sauce*

Serves 4
4 x 175g salmon fillets
salt
16 small new potatoes
8 broccoli florets
2 tbsp olive oil

For the sauce
100g sorrel
260g unsalted butter, plus 1 knob extra
2 shallots, finely diced
1 garlic clove, sliced
1 thyme sprig
1 bay leaf
2 tbsp white wine vinegar
75ml white wine
4 tbsp cream
salt and pepper
1 lemon, halved

Check over the salmon, removing any bones or excess skin.

Bring a pan of salted water to the boil. Scrape the potatoes, add them to the pan and cook until tender.

Meanwhile, start preparing the sauce: remove and discard the tough stalks of the sorrel leaves. Wash the leaves well then spin in a salad spinner until they are dry.

Melt 10g butter in a saucepan, add the sorrel and cook until soft. Purée the mixture in a blender.

Melt a further 10g butter in a heavy-based saucepan. Add the shallots, garlic, thyme and bay leaf, and cook gently for 5 minutes. Pour in the vinegar and allow the liquid to bubble away until the pan is dry. Add the wine, bring to the boil and simmer until it has reduced by half.

Pour in the cream and bring the pan back to the boil. Chop the remaining butter into dice.

Reduce the heat and add the diced butter, whisking continuously until the sauce is hot and molten but do not let it boil.

Season to taste with salt, pepper and lemon juice. Strain the sauce through a fine sieve. Stir in the sorrel purée and keep warm.

In a saucepan of rapidly boiling salted water, cook the broccoli florets until just tender, then drain them and keep hot.

Heat a heavy-based frying pan over a high heat. Brush the cut side of the salmon with olive oil. Carefully place it cut-side down in the dry pan and cook for about a minute, until browned. Be careful: unless the pan is heavy and very hot the salmon will stick and be ruined.

Brush the skin-side with oil and turn the fish over. Cook for another 3 minutes, until the skin is brown and crisp. Remove from the pan.

Drain the potatoes. Add a small knob of butter to the hot pan and toss the potatoes in it until coated.

Place the cooked salmon on the plates skin-side up. Top each portion with 4 new potatoes and 2 broccoli florets. Spoon around the sorrel sauce and serve.

6 meat

You could add some garlic and extra Tabasco but really, says Angela, beef burgers are best kept simple. The additional flavours should come from the fresh ingredients and tasty sauces you layer in the bun. Great for making in advance, these can even be frozen, but make sure you defrost them fully.

beef burgers

Serves 4

600g rump steak

salt and pepper

few drops of Tabasco sauce

olive oil, for brushing

4-6 burger buns, halved

8-12 leaves baby gem lettuce, sliced

1 beef tomato, sliced

1 red onion, sliced in rings

grainy mustard, tomato ketchup, etc.,
  to serve

Tip
Leave the fat on the rump steak so that the burgers are nice and juicy once grilled, and don't grind the meat so much that it becomes rubbery and dry.

Cut the meat roughly into large cubes. Put them in a food processor and blend until the meat is ground but not to a pulp. Season with some salt and pepper and a touch of Tabasco sauce.

Shape the mince into four to six burgers shapes. Put them on a plate and place in the fridge for at least 30 minutes, or until ready to cook.

Preheat the grill. When hot, cook the burgers for 3 minutes on each side, brushing them lightly with a little oil.

Season the cooked burgers with salt and pepper then serve them in the buns with the sliced lettuce, tomato and onion, along with your favourite accompaniments.

more ideas for mince

Minced meats are terrifically versatile and great for feeding the family as well as friends. Go posh with hand-chopped sirloin and gourmet venison, or economical with inexpensive beef cuts shaped into meatballs. The key is to use the right cooking method for your meat.

Chicken burgers

For a tasty chicken burger, mince some fresh chicken and flavour it with chopped parsley, finely chopped shallots, salt, pepper and a little paprika. Fry until the cooked through. Alternatively, why not just enjoy a good grilled chicken breast in a bun with some tarragon-flavoured mayonnaise?

Try lamb and venison

To make lamb burgers, follow the method on the previous page, adding some finely chopped shallots, garlic and fresh coriander. Mint is another good possibility. Or, if you prefer, flavour the lamb with a mixture of chopped fresh rosemary and cumin, then serve the burgers with a spicy apricot chutney, or an aubergine dip such as baba ganoush. Similarly, you can make burgers with veal mince, adding a little sage and serving them with a slice of parma ham between the buns. When using venison mince, try blanched savoy cabbage in place of lettuce and choose a cranberry sauce or onion jelly to accompany.

Steak haché

The French have their own delicious version of beef burgers called steak haché and you can make it at home too. Take a good cut of sirloin, fillet or rump steak (you want it to have a little bit of fat on it) and finely chop it with a large chef's knife for the perfect meaty texture. Bind it with egg and season generously – you could just use salt and pepper, or add some chopped parsley or chilli. Shape into burgers, then fry for 4 minutes on each side so that they have a crunchy brown crust and pink interior. Steak haché is wonderful topped with a fried egg and served with fat hand-cut chips. The advantage is that you know exactly what cut and quality of meat has been put into it.

Onion or not?

Some people add finely chopped onion or shallot to minced beef but leave them out if you enjoy your burger or steak haché medium to rare. The onion won't cook through in the short time it takes to fry the meat and will taste raw and sharp.

Make some meatballs instead

Soak 3 slices of bread in a little milk. Put 400g mince in a large bowl and add 2 finely chopped onions and a finely chopped green chilli. Squeeze the bread dry and add it to the mince with some seasoning. Mix well so that the bread is evenly incorporated.

Shape the mixture into even-sized balls and place on an oiled baking tray. Bake them at 220°C/ gas 7 for 15 minutes until brown and crisp.

Meanwhile, finely chop 2 onions, 2 garlic cloves and a green chilli, and fry them in 20ml olive oil in a casserole until soft. Add 1 tablespoon tomato paste and cook for 2 minutes, then pour in 100ml white wine, bring to the boil and reduce by half.

Stir 500ml chicken stock into the casserole and bring to the boil. Add 2 punnets of cherry tomatoes and season with a pinch of sugar, salt and pepper. Simmer for about 15 minutes.

Tip the browned meatballs into the sauce, then add 10 torn basil leaves. Transfer to the hot oven to continue cooking for another 30 minutes.

Skip the buns

Remember you don't have to serve burgers in buns, it's the meat that should be the star attraction. Instead try burgers with boiled new potatoes, a baked jacket potato, or just a really fresh green salad with tomatoes. You can still enjoy the burger with all your favourite accompaniments such as mayonnaise, chutneys, ketchup, gherkins and so on.

Select your cuts

Unlike beef burgers, meatballs are not cooked medium to rare, and are often cooked a second time in a sauce, so you can choose a cheaper cut of meat, like chuck steak or a lean piece of shin. The same applies when making lamb meatballs: you don't need a prime cut, just one that is not too fatty.

Other ways to serve meatballs

Meatballs are delicious fried until brown then poached in a freshly made, simple tomato sauce. Serve them as is, or for a heartier meal, with some tagliatelle or boiled basmati rice. For a change from tomato sauces, try them with a lovely moist pile of fried onions. Alternatively, do as the Swedes do and pair plain fried or baked meatballs with a choice of tasty fruit jellies and maybe some boiled potatoes.

A frozen asset

Meatballs are a handy way of getting children to eat meat. If you don't want them spicy as in the recipe above, omit the onion and chilli. Make a large quantity and store in batches in the freezer, ready to cook when necessary. Spread the meatballs out on trays to freeze them, then repack in plastic bags or containers. They will defrost quickly but can also be cooked from frozen.

This is a quick version of the traditional Flemish dish beef carbonnade, says John. The quality of the result will depend a great deal on the type of beer you use. Aim for a good organic ale so that it tastes sweet when reduced to a thick meaty sauce – most regions of Britain produce a good one. John likes Badger ales and Thirsty Ferret. Even Newcastle Brown Ale would be delicious here, but avoid bitters and lagers.

beef & ale stew

Serves 2
200g beef fillet tail pieces
salt and pepper
plain flour, for dusting
30g butter
1 onion, sliced
100ml organic ale
tip of 1 bay leaf
pinch of sugar
few drops of Worcestershire sauce
boiled new potatoes, to serve
chopped parsley, to garnish
  (optional)

Cut the beef into 1cm slices. Season them with salt and pepper and dust with flour.

Place a heavy-based skillet pan over a medium heat and melt the butter. Add the beef to the pan and brown it on both sides before transferring to a plate.

In the same pan, cook the onion for 5 minutes, then add them to the beef.

Pour the ale into the skillet to deglaze it. Return the beef and onions to the pan and bring to the boil.

Season with salt and pepper, add the bay leaf and simmer for 20 minutes, or until everything is tender.

Check the seasoning once again, adding a pinch of sugar and a few drops of Worcestershire sauce if desired. Serve with boiled new potatoes. If you feel the stew needs some added colour, then sprinkle over some chopped parsley to serve.

John has a particular fondness for fresh ginger, which is claimed to be an aphrodisiac, and enjoys hot, spicy food. Although not often used in savoury cooking in Europe, ginger features in many Eastern dishes and is handy to have on hand to spike up your cooking. It is rather an unattractive root. Look for crisp specimens – ginger turns bendy when old. Simply break off a piece the size your recipe stipulates and put the rest back in the fridge.

stir-fried beef *with ginger & chilli*

Serves 4

100ml vegetable oil

2 large shallots, chopped

2 garlic cloves, chopped

about 5cm piece ginger, peeled and grated

about 2cm piece galangal, peeled and grated

1 tbsp turmeric powder

2 chillies, deseeded and chopped

60g desiccated coconut

400g brisket, cut into 2cm cubes

100ml coconut cream

salt

coriander leaves and red pepper slices, to garnish (optional)

Heat half the oil in a large, heavy-based pan and cook the shallots, garlic, ginger and galangal gently for a few minutes until lightly coloured.

Stir in the turmeric, chillies and desiccated coconut, and cook for a few minutes more.

In a frying pan or skillet, heat the remaining oil and brown the diced beef in small batches. Add the meat to the spice mixture.

Pour in the coconut cream and 300ml water, and bring to the boil. Simmer uncovered until the meat is almost tender.

Increase the heat slightly and boil to reduce the remaining liquid, stirring continuously. It is ready when the sauce becomes brown, oily and thick – the result should be almost dry. Season with a little salt if required before serving. If you like, garnish with coriander leaves and slices of red pepper.

Tip

Frying pieces of meat in small batches ensures that they brown nicely. Overcrowding the pan makes the meat steam or boil and the colour will not be as mouthwatering.

There is nothing new or unusual about this recipe, says John, but it is often done poorly. Even restaurants make the mistake of using dried herbs, so be sure to add verdant fresh herbs just before serving. It is common to strain out the shallots but John likes to leave them in the sauce for a little texture. Béarnaise works with almost anything that has been roast or grilled, and is particularly lovely with meaty oily fish like salmon and sea bass.

steak *with béarnaise sauce*

Serves 4
4 x 150g beef fillets
salt
vegetable oil, for frying
1 bunch watercress

For the béarnaise sauce
350g butter
2 shallots, finely chopped
8 peppercorns, crushed
1 tarragon sprig
½ bay leaf
1 thyme sprig
1 tbsp tarragon vinegar
1 tbsp dry white wine
3 egg yolks
1 tbsp chopped chervil
1 tbsp chopped chives

Tip

Clarified butter is pure butter fat from which the milk solids and salt have been removed. In addition to its role in sauces, it is favoured by chefs for frying as it does not burn. It will keep for up to two months in the fridge and three in the freezer.

For the sauce, prepare some clarified butter by melting 350g butter in a small, heavy-based saucepan over a low heat. When the butter has started to foam, take it off the heat and leave it to stand for a few minutes so that the milk solids sink to the bottom of the pan. Line a sieve with muslin cloth and pour the butter through it into a bowl: you should have 200g for the béarnaise sauce. Keep it warm in a saucepan.

In a separate small saucepan (do not use an aluminium one), combine the shallots, peppercorns, tarragon sprig, bay leaf, thyme, tarragon vinegar and white wine. Bring to the boil and allow the liquid to reduce to a third of its original volume, being careful not to let it boil dry.

Strain the vinegar mixture into a heatproof bowl, discarding the flavourings.

Place the bowl over a pan of steaming water. Add the egg yolks and whisk over a gentle heat until the mixture is thick and creamy.

Take the bowl off the heat, and slowly whisk in the warm clarified butter, adding a splash of water if the sauce gets too thick. Season the béarnaise with a little salt, stir in the chopped herbs and set aside.

To cook the beef, heat a skillet or frying pan and add a little oil. Season the meat with salt and brown each piece on both sides in the hot pan. Cook to the desired stage: for rare 2½ minutes on each side, for medium 4 minutes on each side, and well-done 6 minutes on each side.

Remove the meat from the pan and drain on kitchen paper. Serve on warm plates with the béarnaise sauce and garnished with watercress.

Escalopes are thin slices of meat cut from the rump of the veal calf. The thinner your escalopes are, the quicker they will cook and the more tender they will be. It's perfectly okay to serve veal pink, says Angela, so there is no need to overcook it. This makes a lovely lunch dish served with salad. If you prefer, substitute flattened chicken or beef for the veal.

veal escalopes

Serves 4

4 veal escalopes

salt and pepper

100g flour

200g breadcrumbs, dried or fresh

1 egg

2 tbsp olive oil

100g butter

1 tbsp chopped parsley

The veal should be about 8mm thick: if the escalopes are any thicker, bat them out evenly with a meat mallet or rolling pin between two sheets of cling film. Season each slice with salt and pepper.

Put the flour and breadcrumbs on separate plates. Beat the egg in a wide low bowl. Working with one escalope at a time, dust both sides in the flour so that they are lightly coated. Dip them in the beaten egg and let the excess drain back into the bowl so that the egg clings to the meat in a fine film. Then lay the escalope in the breadcrumbs and press the crumbs on to each side until the meat is completely coated.

Set aside until ready to cook (they freeze well at this stage, too).

In a large frying pan, heat the olive oil. When hot, cook the veal escalopes on both sides until golden brown.

Add the butter to the pan and cook until it starts to foam.

Just before taking the veal off the heat, add the chopped parsley.

This recipe fuses French techniques with Moroccan flavours. John loves the texture and flavour of chickpeas (sometimes called garbanzos) and says this dish is definitely one to try if you've only ever eaten them puréed in hummus. Chickpeas are done when they are tender but not mushy and, as this recipe uses the pre-cooked canned variety rather than dried, you don't have to worry about them being too crunchy. Flageolet beans would be good here too.

braised lamb, *chickpeas, mint & saffron*

Serves 6

1kg best end of lamb neck fillets

salt and pepper

2 tbsp vegetable oil

30g butter

2 onions, sliced

2 garlic cloves, chopped

*5 tomatoes, skinned, deseeded and
  chopped*

1 tbsp tomato paste

pinch of saffron powder

1.2 litres chicken stock (page 48)

1 x 400g can chickpeas, drained

arrowroot (optional)

1 bunch mint, chopped

100g cooked peas

Cut the lamb into 2cm cubes and season with salt. Heat the oil in a frying pan or skillet and brown the meat in batches. Transfer it to a heavy-based casserole.

Reduce the heat under the pan and add the butter, onions and garlic. Cook until softened, then combine them with the lamb.

Add the tomatoes, tomato paste, saffron and chicken stock to the casserole and bring to the boil. Skim any froth from the surface and leave to simmer, covered, until the lamb is tender, about 45 minutes to 1 hour.

Tip in the chickpeas and bring the casserole back to the boil. Simmer for another 5 minutes and taste for seasoning.

At this stage the stock may be thickened with a little arrowroot if desired: blend about 2 tsp arrowroot with 2 tbsp water and whisk it into the simmering sauce until it is syrupy.

To finish, stir in the mint and cooked peas.

This process seems highly sophisticated, says Angela, but look carefully and you will see it is not very complicated. You could get your butcher to French-trim your lamb for you, but she believes it's a skill worth demystifying.

preparing a rack of lamb

❋❋

2 racks (best end of neck) of lamb

Score along the rib bones about 5-7cm from the tips on both sides of the rack, then cut out the fat and meat between the bones, leaving the tips of the bones exposed.

When purchasing, make sure the butcher removes the chine bone (the backbone), which holds the rack together.
If not, you will need to cut it off vertically with a cleaver. Then, using a sharp knife, cut the layer of skin and fat from the top side of the joint.

Remove the half-moon shaped strip of cartilage at the thinner end of the joint, taking care not to cut into the flesh.

Trim the fat covering the eye of meat so that it is no more than 2mm or so thick. Score the thin strip of fat along the base of the rib bones in a criss-cross fashion.

A best end of lamb contains seven to nine ribs on each side. Cut down halfway along each rack to give four portions of three or four bones each.

Scrape the protruding bones with the knife so that they are as clean as possible. You want to remove every last trace of connective tissue, fat and flesh.

Cut away the line of cream-coloured sinew between the fat and meat lying underneath the ribs.

Alternatively you can cut down between each rib to give individual chops, or pairs of chops, depending on your dish.

Spring is the ideal time to enjoy this dish, says Angela, as that is when new lamb comes into season. The small eyes of meat in the rack should be moist and tender, but cooking them to medium is perfectly acceptable – rare can be a little chewy. Ratatouille tastes best the day after making, so feel free to prepare it in advance, or better still make a large batch. Then you can enjoy extras as a salad, or serve it hot on toast, which will soak up the tasty juices.

rack of lamb *with ratatouille*

Serves 4

a little olive oil, for frying

1 rosemary sprig

2 thyme sprigs

2 garlic cloves, crushed

knob of butter

2 racks (best end of neck) of lamb, trimmed and cut into 4 portions

For the ratatouille

4 tbsp olive oil

2 onions, chopped

3 red peppers, deseeded and diced

3 yellow peppers, deseeded and diced

1 aubergine, diced

4 plum tomatoes, diced

salt and pepper

pinch of sugar (optional)

handful of basil leaves, shredded

Preheat the oven to 200°C/gas 6.

To make the ratatouille, heat the oil in a saucepan and sauté the onion over a medium heat for a few minutes without colouring.

Add the red and yellow peppers and continue to cook for about 5-6 minutes, so that they soften without colouring. Add the aubergine and continue cooking for another 5 minutes.

Stir in the diced tomatoes and season the mixture to taste, adding a little sugar to sweeten if necessary.

Continue cooking the ratatouille over a medium heat for about 30 minutes so that the tomatoes reduce and you have a lovely thick ragout.

Meanwhile, heat a touch of oil in a non-stick frying pan. Add the rosemary, thyme and garlic, followed by the butter, and cook until the butter is foaming and golden brown.

Cover the lamb bones with foil. Put the racks in the frying pan and sear the meat in the flavoured oil for 1-2 minutes on each side, basting with the juices.

If the frying pan is ovenproof, transfer it to the hot oven. Otherwise put the lamb in a roasting tin and roast for approximately 5 minutes.

Remove the lamb from the oven and allow it to rest for at least 15 minutes, leaving the oven on.

Once the meat has rested, reheat it in the oven for 3 minutes. Stir the shredded basil into the ratatouille and serve with the lamb.

Angela says these lamb chops are as delicious served cold as they are hot.
Parmesan cheese is mixed into the crumb coating for a taste of Italy. You
could add a touch of lemon juice to the pan when frying for extra flavour.
Salsa verde is a tangy green herb sauce that makes a vibrant, healthy alternative to butter and cream sauces. It works well with poultry and grilled fish
of all types, and can be stirred into cooked lentils and beans to add pep.

lamb parmigiana *with salsa verde*

Serves 4
8 small lamb chops
1 egg, beaten
salt and pepper
100g plain flour
50g parmesan cheese, finely grated
100g breadcrumbs
50ml olive oil
knob of butter

For the salsa verde
2 tbsp white wine vinegar
4-5 basil sprigs, leaves picked
handful of flat-leaf parsley
2 garlic cloves, chopped
2 anchovy fillets, drained
3 tbsp capers
100ml extra virgin olive oil

Preheat the oven to 200°C/gas 6.

To make the salsa verde, pour the vinegar into a blender then add the
basil leaves, parsley, garlic, anchovies and capers. Blend to a purée.
With the motor still running, gradually add just enough of the olive oil to
give a sauce-like consistency. Set aside until ready to use.

Place each lamb chop between two sheets of cling film and, using a
rolling pin, lightly bash the meat out so that it is 5mm thick.

Beat the egg in a wide bowl and season with salt and pepper. Put the
flour on a plate and season it too. Put the parmesan and breadcrumbs
together on another plate and stir them together.

Dust the lamb chops evenly in the flour, then dip them in the beaten
egg. Coat each chop with the breadcrumbs, shaking off any excess.

Heat the olive oil and butter together in a non-stick frying pan. Fry the
lamb over a medium heat for a few minutes on each side until golden
brown.

Transfer the meat to the oven and continue to cook for a further 1-2
minutes, basting with the pan juices as necessary.

To serve, spoon the salsa verde on the centre of each serving plate and
arrange the lamb chops to one side.

You can't beat lamb with rosemary and garlic, says Angela, the three flavours work fantastically well together. This is another good way of serving lamb at a dinner party, because it looks more extravagant than it really is. You can make the crust well in advance of serving and store it in the freezer for convenience. It can also be used for fish.

herb-crusted rack of lamb

Serves 4

2 tbsp olive oil

2 racks (best end of neck) of lamb, french-trimmed

100g butter

1-2 tsp dijon mustard

For the herb crust

large handful of flat-leaf parsley, coarsely chopped

1 thyme sprig, roughly chopped

4 garlic cloves, crushed

3 rosemary sprigs, roughly chopped

handful of breadcrumbs

For the vinaigrette

5 tbsp olive oil

2 tbsp balsamic vinegar

salt

For the vegetables

6-8 cherry tomatoes

olive oil

pepper

pinch of thyme leaves

4 baby fennel, cut in half at an angle

knob of butter

2 baby courgettes, sliced at an angle

1-2 basil sprigs, leaves torn

Preheat the oven to 170°C/gas 3.

Make the herb crust: in a food processor, combine the parsley, thyme, 2 crushed garlic cloves, and 2 chopped rosemary sprigs and blend to a pulp. Add the breadcrumbs and pulse together briefly. Tip the breadcrumb mixture on to a tray and set aside.

To make the vinaigrette, whisk the olive oil, balsamic vinegar and salt together in a small bowl and set aside.

To prepare the vegetables, cut the cherry tomatoes in half through the centre. Spread them out on a baking tray, drizzle with a little olive oil, season with salt and pepper, and sprinkle the thyme leaves over. Cook in the oven for 30 minutes, until semi-dry.

Preheat the oven to 250°C/gas 9.

To cook the lamb, heat the oil in a non-stick frying pan and add the butter. Allow the butter to foam. Place the lamb in the pan along with the remaining rosemary and garlic and sear for 2 minutes on each side, until browned. As it is searing, baste the meat with the pan juices and cover the bones with foil.

Transfer the lamb to the oven and roast for 4-5 minutes. Then remove the lamb from the oven and allow it to rest for 5 minutes.

Once the lamb has rested, brush it with the dijon mustard and roll the flesh in the breadcrumb mixture to coat. Return to the oven for a further 4-5 minutes, then remove and allow to rest again.

While the lamb is cooking, cook the vegetables. Heat a little oil in a frying pan and lightly cook the fennel with 50-100ml water and a knob of butter for a few minutes to soften.

Add the courgettes and continue cooking for 2-3 minutes, until softened. Transfer the vegetables to a bowl, add the semi-dried tomatoes and a drizzle of the vinaigrette. Stir in a few torn basil leaves.

To serve, spoon the vegetables on to the centre of the serving plates. Carve the lamb into cutlets and arrange on top. Drizzle lightly with the remaining vinaigrette and serve.

Here is a glamorous lamb roast that takes you from smart dinner party through to picnics and sandwiches, as it can be served hot or cold. Lamb shoulder is an underrated cut, says Angela, and this is as versatile as it is impressive. Feel free to vary the filling: add more pancetta, or leave it out; try it with thyme instead of parsley; or add some powdered cinnamon and nuts such as almonds or pine kernels for a Moroccan flavour.

stuffed loin of lamb

Serves 4

1 boned saddle of lamb

4 tbsp olive oil

25g butter

1 large maris piper potato, peeled and diced

1 leek, shredded

100g pancetta lardons

1 tbsp chopped parsley

salt and pepper

Preheat the oven to 180°C/gas 4.

Trim all the excess fat and sinew from the lamb. With a sharp knife, remove all the meat from the fat flaps at either side, so that all that is left is a sheet of lamb fat with the two loins.

Use a mallet or rolling pin to bat out all the fat, between two sheets of cling film, so as to make the sheet of fat thinner.

Heat the olive oil and butter in a frying pan. Add the potato and cook over a medium heat until it has coloured. Add the leeks and cook until they are tender.

In a separate frying pan, sauté the pancetta lardons until golden brown, then add them to the potato and leek mixture. Remove from the heat and set aside to cool.

Mix the chopped parsley into the potato mixture and season well.

Spoon the stuffing into the gap between the two lamb loins. Lay the fillets of lamb on top and roll up into a bundle. Tie up with several pieces of butcher's twine, spacing them about 1cm apart and being careful not to bind the meat too tightly.

Put the rolled joint on a roasting tray. Smear it with olive oil and season well. Cook in the oven for 35 minutes, then remove and leave to rest for at least 10 minutes before slicing.

Anchovies are very salty, whether they are packed in oil or salt. John favours Provençale anchovies packed in sunflower oil (the flavour of olive oil is rather intrusive), which only need to be pat dry with kitchen paper before use. Based on a classic French veal dish, this needs nothing other than a green salad to serve it with, but you could quickly wilt some washed spinach in a saucepan with a little butter to serve alongside if preferred.

escalope of pork *with anchovies*

Serves 4

4 x 100g pork escalopes

plain flour, for dusting

2 eggs, beaten, plus 4 whole eggs

200g breadcrumbs

100ml sunflower oil

knob of butter

salt and pepper

8 anchovy fillets

1 tbsp chopped parsley

If necessary, make the pork escalopes thinner by batting them between two sheets of cling film using a meat mallet or rolling pin.

Dust them in the flour, patting off any excess. Pass them through the beaten eggs, allowing any excess to drip off, and immediately dip into the breadcrumbs. Press well on both sides so that the escalopes are coated with breadcrumbs and set aside on a tray.

Heat half the oil in a large frying pan and brown the escalopes on one side over a steady heat.

Meanwhile, heat the remaining oil in a small frying pan and crack in the eggs. Add a little butter, season with salt and pepper.

Turn the escalopes to brown them on the second side, then drain on kitchen paper.

Position the fried eggs on top of the escalopes. Criss-cross each escalope with two anchovy fillets, sprinkle with parsley and serve.

Variation For a lighter version of this dish, leave out the fried eggs and instead of laying the anchovy fillets on top of the escalopes, chop them finely and stir them into the breadcrumbs before coating the pork escalopes.

Mustard and spices add complexity to the glaze for this suckling pork dish accompanied by a freshly made sauce of buttery prunes, vegetables and sherry vinegar. The good news, says Angela, is that it can all be prepared well in advance, and even served at room temperature rather than hot. Many people are nervous about undercooking pork, but don't let it get too dry either. it should be pink and moist inside.

pork *with honey glaze*

Serves 4

½ loin of suckling pig

handful of rock salt

3 sage leaves

50ml olive oil

For the prune chutney

½ onion

½ leek

½ celery stick

25g butter

20 prunes, chopped

salt and pepper

1 tbsp sherry vinegar

For the honey glaze

150ml honey

1 tbsp dijon mustard

1 tsp mixed spice

1 tsp ground cinnamon

50ml white wine

50ml white wine vinegar

The day before you want to cook, with a sharp knife, cut off all the excess fat and sinew from the pork. Score the skin at 5mm intervals, then repeat crossways.

Rub the skin with the rock salt and leave to sit overnight in the fridge.

Next day, preheat the oven to 180°C/gas 4. Rub off some of the salt and lay the sage leaves down the centre of the flesh side.

Tie the pork with several pieces of butcher's twine, spacing them about 1cm apart and being careful not to tie the meat too tightly. Very lightly smear the joint with olive oil and roast in the oven for 20-30 minutes.

While the pork is cooking, start making the chutney: cut the onion, leek and celery into tiny dice.

Heat the butter in a saucepan, add the vegetables and cook over a medium heat until they are nice and golden. Add the prunes and work with a kitchen spoon so that they break up.

Season the prune mixture well and deglaze the pan with the sherry vinegar. Remove from the heat and set aside.

Make the glaze: in a small saucepan, bring the honey to a boil. Add the mustard and all the spices. Pour in the white wine, followed by the white wine vinegar. Return the glaze to the boil and add some seasoning.

About 10 minutes before the pork is due to finish cooking, pour the honey glaze over the skin and continue roasting.

Once the pork is cooked, remove it from the oven. Leave it to rest for 10 minutes and serve together with the prune chutney.

Tip

Don't be afraid to cut quite deeply into the pork skin when scoring it. This will ensure the crackling cooks evenly and turns out really crunchy.

Rhubarb makes a change from the well known sweet-sour combination of pork and apples, but you could also use gooseberries or plums in this dish if prefererred. If you don't want to miss out on crackling, says John, roast it in a pan alongside, then cut it up and serve a piece on each plate.

loin of pork *with walnut crust & rhubarb*

Serves 6

4 strips lemon zest

1.75kg pork loin, skin removed

2 garlic cloves, sliced

1 tbsp chopped parsley

salt

20ml vegetable oil

100g walnuts

100g breadcrumbs

50g soft butter

400g rhubarb, cut into 5cm batons

200g caster sugar

300ml white wine

300ml chicken stock (page 48)

1 savoy cabbage, quartered and core removed

Preheat the oven to 190°C/gas 5.

Bring a small saucepan of water to the boil, add the strips of lemon zest and cook for 1 minute. Drain and refresh under cold running water, then shred the lemon zest.

With a small pointed knife, make several incisions in the pork. Into each incision poke a little shredded lemon zest, garlic and parsley. Season with salt.

Heat the oil in a roasting pan and, when it is smoking-hot, lay the pork in the pan fat-side down. Cook, turning, to brown evenly, then transfer to the hot oven to roast for 30 minutes.

Remove the pan from the oven and tip off any fat. Pour in the wine and continue roasting for 40 minutes.

Meanwhile, in a food processor, whiz the walnuts and breadcrumbs together to give fine crumbs. Add the butter and whiz again, just enough to form a soft paste.

Take the pork out of the oven again. Tip the cooking juices into a saucepan and set aside. Press the walnut paste on to the fat so that it is evenly coated.

Return the pork to the oven and reduce the oven temperature to 140°C/gas 1. Continue cooking until the crust is brown.

While the pork is cooking, put the rhubarb in an ovenproof dish and sprinkle with the sugar and add a little water. Place in the oven to bake until tender.

Cook the cabbage wedges in a large pan of boiling salted water until tender. Drain and, while still hot, shred the cabbage. Keep to one side.

Bring the cooking juices to a fast boil and reduce to concentrate the flavours.

Reheat the cabbage in a little of the sauce and season with salt and pepper, if required.

To serve, carefully position two batons of rhubarb on each plate and share out the hot cabbage. Slice the pork and place it on the plate just off-centre, leaning against the cabbage. Spoon around the sauce.

Variation For a simpler version of this dish, leave out the walnut crust and cabbage.

The marriage of red cabbage and venison is delicious, says Angela, and this dish really doesn't need any further accompaniments. If you are using wild venison in season, it can be gamey but the cabbage is robust enough to stand up to it. Farmed venison is readily available year-round and has a milder taste. You can keep the venison in the marinade for as long as three or four days, which will tenderize it as well as add a rich flavour.

venison *with braised red cabbage*

Serves 4
3 tbsp vegetable oil
50-125g butter
4 x 150g venison loins

For the braised cabbage
1 small red cabbage, thinly sliced
1 clove
½ cinnamon stick
375ml port
5 tbsp red wine vinegar
75g duck fat
1 small onion, thinly sliced
1 braeburn apple, peeled and sliced

Start preparing the red cabbage the day before: put it in a non-corrosive container and add the clove and cinnamon. Cover with the port and red wine vinegar and leave to marinate in the fridge overnight.

Next day, heat the duck fat in a large saucepan or casserole, add the sliced onion and cook until lightly coloured.

Drain the cabbage, reserving the marinade. Add the cabbage to the onion and cook over a medium heat for 10 minutes, stirring occasionally.

Add the apple to the cabbage mixture, then pour in the reserved port marinade. Bring to the boil and simmer over a medium heat for 45 minutes or until the cabbage offers very little resistance to the bite.

Meanwhile, preheat the oven to 200°C/gas 6.

Place a frying pan on the stove and when it is hot, add the vegetable oil. Once the oil is hot, add the butter and allow it to foam.

Season the venison loins with salt and pepper. Add them to the pan and cook until coloured on each side. Lay the venison in the pan and cook until coloured on all sides.

Transfer the venison to the hot oven and roast for 3 minutes. Set aside to rest for 5 minutes before serving it with the braised red cabbage.

7

pasta
& grains

Here is a lovely way to use summer vegetables, says Angela. Pappardelle is a rustic style of pasta ribbon that can accommodate bold flavours as it is quite thick. In this recipe you will really taste the benefit of using your own fresh pasta, but if you do not have the time to make it, Angela advises buying dried pappardelle rather than a packet of factory-produced 'fresh' pasta. If you would prefer a more delicate dish, substitute tagliatelle.

pappardelle, peas & broad beans

Serves 4

salt and pepper
500g broad beans in the pod
150g podded fresh peas
500g fresh or dried pappardelle
4 tbsp olive oil
3 plum tomatoes

Bring a saucepan of salted water to the boil. Take the broad beans out of their pods and blanch them for 1 minute in the boiling water. Refresh in iced water, then peel the beans and set aside.

In the same pan of boiling water, blanch the peas for 2 minutes, then refresh in iced water and set aside.

Meanwhile, bring a pot of salted water to the boil and cook the pappardelle for 3 minutes if using fresh pasta, or 8-10 minutes if using dried (refer to the packet instructions). When cooked, the pasta should be tender but still have some bite. Drain thoroughly.

Deseed the tomatoes, but don't peel them, then cut the flesh into strips.

Heat the olive oil in a wide frying pan. Add the peas and broad beans and cook over a medium heat until the vegetables are heated through. Season to taste with salt and pepper.

Add the drained pasta. Toss well, then add the tomato strips. Adjust the seasoning to taste and serve.

This simple dish of pasta ribbons and meaty mushrooms is a classic Italian combination, but you may be surprised how versatile it can be. Angela recommends substituting ingredients according to whatever you have available, using, for example, dried wild mushrooms instead of fresh, the assertive favour of sage leaves instead of parsley, or a piece of streaky bacon in lieu of pancetta. Best of all, it can be on the table in around 20 minutes.

tagliatelle *with mushrooms & pancetta*

Serves 4

200g pancetta, diced

1 garlic clove, crushed

500g mixed wild mushrooms, trimmed and sliced

splash of olive oil

500g dried or fresh tagliatelle

2 tbsp chopped flat-leaf parsley

In a frying pan, sauté the pancetta and garlic until the pancetta is golden. Remove them from the pan and set aside on a plate.

Add the mushrooms to the pan and sauté them in the fat left from cooking the pancetta, adding a little olive oil if necessary.

Meanwhile, bring a pot of salted water to the boil and cook the pasta for 3-4 minutes if using fresh pasta, and 6-7 minutes if using dried. The pasta is done when it is tender but still has a little bite to it.

Drain well, then toss the pasta, pancetta and parsley together with the mushrooms and serve.

Tip

Never rinse cooked pasta, as the starch gives the other ingredients in the dish something to cling to. Instead simply drain and throw it into the pan of sauce. Don't be afraid to add a little of the pasta cooking water to the sauce for a moist result, either.

Carbonara is so often badly done, says Angela, but when it is good it is absolutely delicious. Spaghetti is the traditional type of pasta used, but rigatoni or (better still) penne work very well too, as the sauce coats these shapes quickly and easily – one of the secrets of success in this dish.

spaghetti carbonara

Serves 2
salt and black pepper
200g spaghetti
1 large onion
4 tbsp olive oil
150g pancetta lardons
150ml double cream
4 egg yolks
100g parmesan cheese, grated

Tip
Be sure to pull the pan off the heat before you add the egg yolks to prevent them scrambling. This is one dish that really needs to be served promptly, too.

Bring a pot of salted water to the boil. Add the spaghetti and cook according to the packet instructions (usually 7-10 minutes), being careful not to overcook the pasta. When it is tender but still has some bite, drain it thoroughly.

While the pasta is cooking, chop the onion. Heat the olive oil in a frying pan, add the onion and cook over a medium-high heat until it is just beginning to colour.

In a separate pan, fry the pancetta until golden brown, then add it to the onion.

Pour in the cream, bring the sauce to the boil and season with salt. Remove the pan from the heat.

Add the drained spaghetti to the sauce, followed by the egg yolks and parmesan and mix well together.

Serve straight away with plenty of freshly ground black pepper.

A good staple pasta dish for quick midweek suppers, this is made quickly from ingredients most people keep in the fridge and cupboard as a matter of course, says Angela. It is also a great one for serving to children. If you prefer, use the chopped tail end of a piece of salami instead of pancetta.

tomato & bacon *penne*

Serves 4

salt and pepper
500g penne
1 punnet cherry tomatoes
1 garlic clove
1 red chilli
1 bunch spring onions
3 basil leaves
100g pancetta lardons
50ml white wine
100ml fresh tomato sauce ot passata

Bring a pot of salted water to the boil. Add the penne and cook according to the packet instructions (usually 8-10 minutes), being careful not to overcook it. When the pasta is tender but still has some bite, drain it thoroughly.

While the pasta is cooking, cut the cherry tomatoes in half. Slice the garlic, then finely shred the chilli, spring onions and basil.

Heat a frying pan, add the pancetta and cook, stirring often, until just golden brown. Drain the excess fat from the pan.

Return the pan to the heat and add the garlic, chilli, and spring onions. Add some salt and pepper, and cook until lightly coloured.

Add the cherry tomatoes and cook over high heat for 2-3 minutes. Deglaze the pan with the white wine and leave to cook for 5 minutes.

Add the tomato sauce and bring the pan to the boil. Season to taste with salt and pepper.

Tip the drained penne into the sauce. Add the shredded basil, stir gently and serve.

You need to take your time making lasagne, says Angela. This is a dish that cannot be rushed, but once finished it is a complete meal in itself. Good bolognese and béchamel sauces are essential, though if you want to make it for vegetarians, using ratatouille instead of bolognese is equally tasty.

lasagne

Serves 6

For the bolognese sauce
700g beef topside
300g veal topside
1 carrot
1 large onion
2 celery sticks
2 garlic cloves
50ml vegetable oil
salt and pepper
1 tbsp tomato paste
1 bay leaf
4 thyme sprigs
100ml red wine
100ml white wine
150ml canned crushed tomatoes
250ml chicken stock (page 48)
250ml veal stock

For the béchamel sauce
40g butter
40g flour
400-500ml milk

For layering
1 packet lasagne sheets, 10cm square
200g parmesan, grated

Tip
Make sure every bit of pasta is covered with sauce, especially on the top layer, so that it does not dry out in the oven.

To make the bolognese sauce, dice all the meat and finely chop the vegetables and garlic.

Heat the vegetable oil in a large frying pan. Brown the meat in small batches, so that it sizzles and fries rather than boils or stews.

Once all the meat is coloured, add the vegetables and garlic and cook together for 5 minutes.

Season well with salt and pepper, stir in the tomato paste, then add the bay leaf and thyme.

Deglaze the pan with the red and white wines. Once it has evaporated, add the tomatoes and cook, stirring occasionally, until the tomatoes have broken down and the liquid evaporated.

Pour in the chicken and veal stocks and cook over a low heat for 15-20 minutes, or until the meat is just tender and the mixture is thick and saucy. Check the seasoning and discard the herbs.

While that is cooking, make the béchamel sauce, melt the butter in a saucepan then add the flour. Cook, stirring, over a medium heat for a few minutes.

Add about one-third of the milk to the pan and whisk together until smooth. Pour in the rest of the milk and mix well. Season generously with salt and pepper, and leave the sauce to simmer over a medium heat, stirring occasionally, for 15 minutes.

Cook the sheets of pasta in boiling salted water according to the packet instructions. Refresh the cooked pasta in iced water. Oil a few sheets of cling film or parchment paper and stack the pasta in layers using the cling film or paper to divide them.

Preheat the oven to 180°C/gas 4.

Spread a thin layer of béchamel sauce in a large rectangular or square ovenproof dish. Cover with a layer of pasta, then one of Bolognese sauce. Smooth over another layer of béchamel, then sprinkle with some parmesan. Repeat the layers again, starting with the pasta, and continue with the remaining ingredients. The last layer should be pasta covered with a thin coating of béchamel and a final sprinkling of cheese.

Cover the dish with foil and bake for 20 minutes, or until the lasagne is hot in the centre and bubbling at the sides. Discard the foil, press down around the sides of the lasagne with a spoon and continue baking for a further 5 minutes so that the parmesan colours.

The secret to Angela's golden yellow pasta dough is the eggs – she buys Italian ones produced by chickens who feed on corn and carrots. Look out for them, and authentic '00' pasta flour, in speciality delicatessens.

making fresh pasta

Makes about 1kg
600g '00' pasta flour
¼-½ tsp salt
5-6 large country eggs
1 tbsp olive oil
semolina, for sprinkling

Gradually draw the flour into the eggs, mixing steadily to make a coarse paste. Add more of the egg mixture as needed.

Tip the pasta flour on to a clean work surface and sprinkle with the salt. Make a well in the centre of the flour. Beat the eggs and olive oil together and pour two-thirds of the mixture into the well.

Keep working the dough with your hands, gradually bringing it together to form a ball.

Knead for 10 minutes, or until the dough is very smooth and elastic.

When the dough is silky smooth, shape it into a ball. Wrap tightly with cling film and leave to rest in the fridge for at least 30 minutes.

Dust the work surface lightly with flour. Use a rolling pin to roll your first piece of dough out into a rectangle, so that it can fit through the machine.

Use the heel of your hand and your upper body weight to push the dough out along the work surface, then fold the dough back and press down on it with your knuckles. Give it a half turn and repeat, using a rhythmic motion. This process helps develops the gluten in the flour.

Clean your work surface, then, when you are ready to roll out the dough, cut it into manageable pieces and work with one piece at a time, keeping the rest of the dough covered with cling film or a damp cloth.

Adjust the machine to the widest setting and slowly guide the pasta dough through it, cranking the handle to feed it through. Do not try and force the dough through the machine, or pull it out. Fold the dough into three and run it through again on this wide setting.

When the pasta dough is flat, pick it up and fold it in three so that it will fit through the opening in the pasta machine.

Decrease the setting on the pasta machine by one notch and roll the sheet of pasta through again, but without folding the dough first. Ease the pasta gently from the machine and across the work surface, then feed it through once more on this setting.

Decrese the setting on the pasta machine again by one notch and repeat the double rolling process, using your hands to support the pasta sheet so that it does not tear as it lengthens. If the pasta begins to stick, dust it lightly with flour, being careful not to use too much.

When the dough is very thin (about 1-2mm) and silky, lay it over the work surface and cut into pieces about 25cm long. The machine has a choice of settings for producing pasta ribbons: just select one and feed the dough through it.

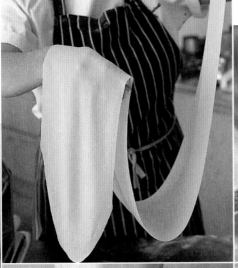

Spread the cut pasta out on the work surface or on traysand allow it to rest and dry out for at least 20 minutes before cooking.

Continue rolling the pasta through the machine, decreasing the setting gradually and running the dough through the machine twice on each setting. Dust it lightly with flour whenever you feel it is necessary to prevent sticking.

Alternatively, a pasta wheel with a zigzagged edge will give a professional fluted edge. Various rollers and shaped cutters are also available for cutting pasta, but you can also use a knife, or cookie cutters. For tagliattelle, cut the ribbons about 1.2cm wide, for pappardelle, 2.5cm wide.

Dust the cut pasta with semolina to prevent sticking. Semolina is coarse, so the pasta will not absorb it as it would fine flour. In this way, if necessary, the pasta can be left for up to 24 hours before cooking.

This is a traditional dish of Emilia-Romagna, home to many of Italy's most famous ingredients, including parmigiano-reggiano cheese (the finest parmesan), parma ham and balsamic vinegar. Angela recommends making a large batch of tortelli in one hit and freezing them to serve on future dates. They cook well straight from frozen. Use swiss chard instead of spinach if desired, which will give an extra bite.

spinach & ricotta tortelli

Serves 4

400g spinach

150g ricotta

pinch of grated nutmeg

50g breadcrumbs

75g parmesan cheese, grated, plus
   extra to serve

salt and freshly ground black pepper

500g fresh pasta dough (page 160)

1 egg, beaten

extra virgin olive oil, for drizzling

Tip
Buy a good organic ricotta and make sure the balance between it and the volume of cooked spinach is even.

Cook the spinach in a large saucepan with 2 tablespoons water for about 3 minutes, or until it wilts. Drain the spinach in a colander and squeeze out all the excess moisture with your hands. Chop the spinach finely, then place it in a bowl and leave it to cool.

Add the ricotta to the spinach and mix together. Add the nutmeg, breadcrumbs, parmesan and some salt and pepper. Refrigerate this mixture until you're ready to fill the tortelli.

Roll out the pasta dough following the instructions on pages 160-163, then cut the rolled dough into 2cm squares.

Fill the tortelli by placing 1 teaspoon of filling in the centre of half the pasta squares. Brush the edges lightly with beaten egg, then cover with the remaining pasta squares to make little parcels. Trim the edges with a cutter to seal and crimp.

At this stage you can par-cook the tortelli to serve later. Bring a large pan of salted water to the boil, add the tortelli and cook for 30 seconds. Drain and plunge the pasta immediately into iced water. Remove and place on a lightly oiled baking sheet.

When almost ready to serve, bring a large pan of salted water to the boil and cook the tortelli for 3 minutes, or until they rise to the surface. Alternatively, if you are cooking the tortelli without par-boiling them, boil for 3-4 minutes, until they rise to the surface of the water.

Drain and serve immediately with a drizzle of extra virgin olive oil and some more grated parmesan.

Angela's sophisticated take on ravioli incorporates exotic Asian flavours of sesame oil, soy sauce, ginger and coriander to counterbalance a rich filling of scallop and salmon mousse. You could use pure salmon, if preferred, or replace the salmon with king prawns for an equally delicious result.

salmon ravioli

Serves 4
500g fresh pasta dough (see page 160)
1 egg, beaten
splash of olive oil

For the filling
100g king scallop meat, or 2-3 king
* scallops (200-250g), shelled and*
* cleaned*
about 100g double cream
600g salmon fillet, skinned and diced
few coriander leaves, chopped
few basil leaves, chopped
squeeze of lemon juice

For the dressing
1 tbsp soy sauce
4 tbsp sesame oil
2 tbsp balsamic vinegar
2.5cm piece of ginger, peeled and
* sliced*
salt and pepper

To serve
1 tbsp olive oil
150g spinach leaves
1-2 sprigs basil, leaves torn
1 sprig dill, chopped
1 sprig flat-leaf parsley, chopped
3-4 pinches micro-cresses (optional)

To make the filling: put the scallops in a food processor and whiz to give a mince. With the motor running, gradually add the cream until the mixture is smooth. Transfer to a large bowl and stir in the diced salmon pieces, coriander, basil and a squeeze of lemon juice.

To make the dressing, whisk the soy sauce, sesame oil and balsamic vinegar in a bowl. Add the ginger and season to taste.

Roll out the dough to the thinnest setting on the pasta machine, following the instructions on pages 160-163. Cut the sheets into 24 rounds using a cutter.

Spoon the salmon mixture on to the centre of 12 pasta circles, dividing it equally. Brush the edges lightly with beaten egg and place the remaining pasta circles on top.

Press together to seal the edges. Trim the edges of the ravioli with scissors or a cutter. You need 12 ravioli to serve three per person. Save the leftover pasta for use another day.

Bring a pot of salted water to the boil, adding a little olive oil to prevent sticking. Cook the pasta for 3½ minutes, then drain.

Meanwhile, to prepare to serve, heat a little olive oil in a small saucepan and wilt the spinach for 1-2 minutes, adding seasoning to taste. Drain the spinach.

To serve, arrange the wilted spinach into the centre of each serving plate. Place the salmon ravioli on top and drizzle with the dressing. Scatter with a few torn herb leaves and micro-cresses to garnish.

There is no mystery to producing perfectly fluffy rice, says John, and this simple cooking method is best. Use basmati rice for its neutral yet naturally nutty flavour that will be a perfect contrast to strongly flavoured curries.

boiled basmati rice

Serves 4
100g basmati rice
salt

Wash the rice in a bowl of water, or by placing it in a sieve under the tap, then drain it thoroughly.

Bring a large pan of salted water to the boil and rain in the rice. Stir briefly to prevent the rice settling on the bottom, then bring the water back to the boil.

Cook at a fast pace, but not a full boil, for about 12-15 minutes, or until the rice is tender.

Drain in a sieve and run hot tap water over the rice to wash away any excess starch.

Serve at once, or set aside and reheat later in a steamer or microwave.

Here John has produced an easy Western version of a classic street food dish of Indonesia and Malaysia. It makes a great supper dish, perfect for eating with a fork in front of the telly. You can use pork instead of chicken.

nasi goreng

4 tbsp sesame oil

2 onions, finely chopped

1 red chilli, deseeded and finely chopped

2 garlic cloves, crushed

200g smoked streaky bacon, diced

100g cold cooked chicken

100g prawns

splash of vegetable oil

2 eggs

250g cooked rice

100g sweetcorn kernels

2 tbsp plum sauce

1 tbsp soy sauce

Warm the sesame oil in a large pan and gently cook the onions, chilli and garlic together until soft.

Add the bacon, turn up the heat and cook quickly, stirring often. Add the chicken and prawns, and continue cooking for 2 minutes, stirring continuously.

Meanwhile, heat a small frying pan over a moderate heat, adding a little oil. Beat the eggs until smooth and pour them into the pan. Cook like a big, flat pancake, without letting the eggs colour. Turn to cook the other side briefly.

When the egg is done, tip it out on to a work surface. Roll it up like a cigar or swiss roll, then slice it thinly.

Add the cooked rice, sweetcorn, plum sauce and soy sauce to the chicken and prawn mixture and allow to heat through, tossing well to combine. Taste for seasoning and correct if required.

Serve with the shredded egg sprinkled on top.

Why use a sheet of greaseproof paper to cover this pilaf instead of a pan lid? If you seal the pan with a lid, says John, the steam cannot escape, which produces a soggy result. With the buttered circle of paper (known to chefs as a cartouche), enough liquid is retained in the pan to prevent the rice burning, but evaporation also occurs, giving a beautifully fluffy texture.

rice pilaf

150g butter
2 onions, finely chopped
500g basmati rice
1 cinnamon stick
3 star anise
16 cloves
1 tsp cumin seeds
1 tsp coriander seeds
12 cardamom pods
2 bay leaves
1 thyme sprig
2 strips orange zest
2 strips lemon zest
800ml chicken stock (page 48)
salt and pepper

Preheat the oven to 180°C/gas 4.

Melt the butter in a casserole, add the onions and cook for a couple of minutes to soften.

Add the rice, mixing well so that the grains are coated with the melted butter, then add the spices, herbs and citrus zest, and mix well.

Pour in the chicken stock and bring to the boil. Cover with a circle of buttered greaseproof paper.

Transfer the rice to the oven for 18 minutes. When done, remove the casserole from the oven, and lightly fork through the rice to loosen the grains before serving.

A hearty, satisfying dish perfect for the cold months of winter, pumpkin risotto can be given a dash of restaurant glamour with a garnish of deep-fried sage leaves. Angela insists that making risotto is simple once you have mastered the knack, but it does take some mastering. Give yourself a head start by using a good-quality stock for cooking the rice, and making no attempt to rush the cooking process. A kitchen timer will prove invaluable.

pumpkin risotto

Serves 4

800ml-900ml chicken or vegetable
  stock (page 48)
2 tbsp olive oil
1 shallot, chopped
250g carnaroli or arborio rice
75ml white wine
75g parmesan cheese, grated
75-100g cold butter, diced

For the pumpkin purée
50g butter
400g pumpkin, diced
salt and pepper

First make the pumpkin purée. Melt the butter in a saucepan, add the pumpkin and cook over a medium heat until it starts to break down, making sure it doesn't colour.

Add some seasoning and continue cooking over a low heat, until the pumpkin is completely soft. Blitz the mixture with a hand blender until completely smooth and set aside.

While the pumpkin is cooking, heat the stock for the risotto in a small saucepan until it is piping hot.

In a separate pan, heat the olive oil and fry the shallot over a medium heat until it is cooked but not coloured. Add the rice and cook, stirring, until it starts to become translucent.

Deglaze the pan of rice with the wine and set a timer for 20 minutes. As soon as the wine has evaporated, start ladling in the hot stock, one ladleful at a time, stirring constantly. The pan should contain just enough liquid to be bubbling, without the rice swimming in stock.

When there is 5 minutes remaining on the timer, let the rice dry off a bit.

Add 100g pumpkin purée (keep the rest to reheat as a side dish) and some seasoning, and continue cooking and stirring. Add more stock only if necessary – the consistency of the rice should be creamy and on the dry side at this stage.

When there is only 2 minutes left on the timer, add the parmesan and diced butter. Remove the pan from the heat and keep stirring the rice with a wooden spoon to develop the creamy consistency. Add some extra stock if needed - the rice should be of a consistency that it runs a bit when poured on to a plate. Serve immediately.

risotto variations

Risotto can be served as a starter, as a dinner party main course or enjoyed as a simple supper. Although it requires careful attention to coax the starch from the grains, the stirring process can be quite relaxing. Here are some ideas to inspire your own creativity.

Switch the purée

Once you've got the knack of making risotto with a vegetable purée such as the pumpkin one overleaf, it is a straightforward matter to produce other versions simply by changing the purée. Try using carrots and finish the risotto with some chopped fresh chervil.

Mushroom and mascarpone risotto

Cook the rice base as described on the previous page using 3 tablespoons olive oil to fry 2 finely diced medium shallots, then stirring in 200g arborio rice. Pour 100ml dry white wine into the oil-coated rice, then gradually add 600ml hot chicken stock, stirring gently. In another frying pan, melt 25g butter and quickly fry 100g quartered button mushrooms. When the rice is cooked, season it to taste, then stir in the mushrooms, plus 2 tablespoons mascarpone cheese and 1 tablespoon chopped chives. Spoon on to warmed plates and sprinkle with 25g grated parmesan cheese.

Rabbit risotto

To make a rabbit risotto, take a couple of rabbit legs and braise them slowly in the oven in enough chicken or vegetable stock to cover, plus a sprig of rosemary. You'll need to cook them for about 1½ hours at 180°C/gas 4.

When the meat is cooked and cool enough to handle, shred it. Use the braising liquid as your stock (taste it – you may want first to reduce it by boiling to strengthen the flavour).

Make your risotto base and, about 5 minutes before the rice is cooked, add the shredded rabbit meat and allow it to warm through.

Great ways to garnish

A small handful of fresh rocket leaves and a few shavings of good quality parmesan cheese (look for the term 'parmigiano reggiano' on the pack) works best on almost all occasions. Alternatively, try some pieces of crisp fried pancetta, or a few roast prawns.

Make leftovers into arancini

In Italy leftover risotto is made into arancini, a savoury snack that originated in Sicily but is now sold everywhere. The name means 'little oranges', which is what they look like once cooked.

To make them, take some cold risotto and, using wet hands, shape it into balls of the same size (you may like to add a beaten egg to the mixture first). Make a hollow in each ball and fill it with some beef ragu. If desired, you could also add a couple of cubes of cheese. Smooth the rice mixture over the filling so that it is completely enclosed.

Coat the rice balls with flour, beaten egg and finally breadcrumbs as described for risotto cakes on the right.

Fill a deep-fryer with vegetable oil and, once hot, fry the arancini in batches until orangey-brown. Drain and serve hot, or warm.

Tips for green vegetable risottos

When making risotto with green vegetables like peas or diced courgettes, add them to the risotto base about 5-8 minutes before serving, not at the very beginning of cooking. An exception is asparagus risotto, for which you should add the chopped stems about halfway through. Keep the tips to serve on top of the risotto, and either blanch them in boiling salted water, or sauté them lightly in a little butter until just tender.

Choose you stock carefully

When making fish or seafood risottos, choose a vegetable stock for preference, as the taste of fish stock can be too powerful once it is concentrated.

Try other cheeses

There is some scope for varying the cheese used in risottos. The Italian sheep's milk variety pecorino is an excellent alternative to parmesan. Pea and gorgonzola is a delicious combination for risotto, too, but make sure you still add a touch of parmesan and butter at the end to help blend the risotto and give it a silky finish.

Risotto cakes

Make risotto cakes by beating an egg and working it into a bowl of cold, leftover risotto. Add a little chopped shallot, chopped parsley and some salt and pepper, then shape the mixture into patties. Dust them lightly in flour, then dip in beaten egg and coat with breadcrumbs. Shallow-fry the cakes in clarified butter until there is a golden crust on each side, then transfer to an oven at 190°C/gas 5 to finish cooking for 5 minutes. Serve with a rocket salad, or with a wild mushroom and cream sauce such as the one featured in the recipe on page 82.

Decent ready-made pastry is readily available in supermarkets, but making your own allows you to add tasty flavourings such as the cheese and poppy seeds used here. This recipe gives enough pastry for two flan cases you could bake one straight away for the flan overleaf and freeze the other.

vegetable couscous

Serves 4

1 large courgette

1 large aubergine

1 red pepper

1 yellow pepper

50ml olive oil, plus extra for frying

2 tsp white wine vinegar

250g couscous

salt and pepper

herb leaves, to garnish (optional)

Cut the courgette in quarters lengthways. Sit each piece on the chopping board skin-side down and trim off most of the flesh. Cut the skin portion into 1cm cubes and set aside. Repeat the process with the aubergine.

Cut the peppers into quarters and discard all the seeds and pith before cutting the flesh into 1cm cubes.

Heat a litte olive oil in a frying pan over a medium-high heat. Add each vegetable in turn and cook, stirring until lightly browned. Remove to a bowl while you continue cooking the other vegetables, adding more olive oil as necessary.

Bring 250ml water to a boil with the vinegar and 50ml olive oil. Sprinkle the couscous over a baking tray. Add some salt and pepper to the hot water, then pour it over the couscous. Cover with cling film and set aside in a warm place for 10-15 minutes.

When the couscous has hydrated, discard the cling film and fluff up the grains with your fingertips or a fork. The couscous should be loose and sandy.

Add the cooked vegetables to the couscous and mix well. Adjust the seasoning to taste and serve, garnished with herb leaves if you like.

vegetables

Nearly everyone's favourite vegetable, potatoes can be crisp and savoury or comfortingly creamy. Here John presents three of the most useful ways of cooking them ready to accompany whatever you fancy.

potato purée

Serves 4
1kg old potatoes, such as king edward or maris piper, peeled
salt and pepper
60ml milk
150g butter
freshly grated nutmeg

Cut the potatoes into even pieces. Put them in a saucepan, cover with cold water and add a pinch of salt. Simmer for 20 minutes, until tender.

Drain the potatoes and return them to the warm pan. Place over a gentle heat to drive off any excess moisture.

Carefully pass the potatoes through a sieve. Meanwhile, warm the milk in a small pan or microwave oven.

Return the puréed potato to the pan and add the butter. Work together over a low heat until smooth. Add the warm milk and season with salt, pepper and nutmeg. Mix well and serve hot.

roast potatoes

Serves 4
4 large desirée or king edward potatoes, peeled and quartered
salt
50ml goose fat or 30g beef dripping

Preheat the oven to 200°C/gas 6.

Put the potatoes in a large saucepan of cold salted water and bring to the boil. Cook over a moderate heat for 6 minutes or until tender.

Meanwhile put your choice of fat in a roasting tray and place in the oven to heat.

Drain the potatoes in a colander. Return them to the saucepan and cover with a lid. Shake the pan to rough up the edges of the potatoes.

Add the potatoes to the hot fat and sprinkle with salt. Roast for 45 minutes, turning occasionally so that the bottoms do not burn.

sautéed potatoes

Serves 4
800g small potatoes, scrubbed
salt
vegetable oil
1 tbsp finely chopped parsley or chives

Choose even-sized potatoes and cook them (with their skins on) in boiling, salted water until tender but not mushy.

Drain the potatoes in a colander and allow them to cool slightly.

With a small knife, peel the potatoes and slice into 1cm pieces.

In a large frying pan, heat a little oil and tip in the potatoes. Allow them to brown on one side before turning. Continue cooking until brown until crisp.

Season with a little salt and sprinkle with the chopped herbs. Serve hot.

When you want to make chips, Angela recommends asking your local fish and chip shop what potato varieties they are currently using, as the best varies seasonally. Remember bigger is not necessarily better: you want a very dry variety, and maris pipers usually fit the bill. Leave the skins on if you like, but make sure they are very clean and dry before frying.

chips

Serves 4
3-4 large maris piper potatoes
groundnut oil for deep-frying
salt and pepper

Decide whether to peel the potatoes or leave the skin on for their flavour. If leaving them on, scrub the skins well. P

Cut the potatoes into chips roughly 10-15mm wide and rinse them under cold running water to remove any excess starch. Pat them dry well in a clean tea towel.

In a deep-fryer, heat the oil to 140°C. If you don't have a suitable thermometer, a small cube of bread will sizzle and turn golden brown in 60 seconds. (Also, don't fill the pan more than one-third fill of oil or it may bubble over when the potatoes are added.)

Once the oil is hot, add a small batch of chips to it - you don't want to add a lot because that will make the temperature of the oil drop. Cook the potatoes until they become soft and are just starting to colour.

Lift the chips from the oil and drain them on kitchen paper while you repeat the frying process with the remaining chips.

At this point you can reserve the part-cooked chips for up to a day, or freeze them for use another time.

When ready to finish cooking the chips, heat the oil to 180°C (a small cube of bread will turn golden brown in 20 seconds). When it is ready, add a batch of chips and fry them until golden brown.

Lift the chips from the oil and leave them to drain on kitchen paper so that all the excess oil gets absorbed. Keep them hot, uncovered (or they lose their crispness) in a low oven with the door ajar while you fry the remaining chips.

When all the chips are cooked, season them well and serve hot.

A popular side dish in Southern Italy, where it is known as zucchine fritte, these battered and fried strips of courgette are a good accompaniment to roast chicken as well as a terrific treat served as a canapé with drinks. If you have access to courgette flowers, they can be deep-fried in the same batter, says Angela, once the pistils have been removed and the petals cleaned.

deep-fried courgettes

Serves 4

4 large courgettes
320g tempura flour (batter mix)
sparkling water
ice cubes
cornflour, for dusting
groundnut oil, for deep-frying
salt and pepper

Tip

Using iced sparkling water and keeping the batter cold helps ensure a really crispy batter and great result.

Cut the courgettes in half lengthways, then in half lengthways again, then cut across to produce pieces about 6cm long and 1cm thick.

Make the tempura batter following the instructions on the packet using ice-cold sparkling water instead of whatever liquid they say. As you blend it (tempura batter suits not being overmixed - a few lumps are fine), sit the bowl of batter over a bowl of ice to ensure it is kept cold.

Heat the oil to 180˚C in a deep-fryer (if you don't have a suitable thermometer, a small cube of bread will sizzle and turn golden brown in 20 seconds. When it is ready, dust the courgette wedges with cornflour and dip them in the batter.

Working in batches and using tongs or a slotted spoon, transfer them from the batter to the oil and cook until golden brown all over.

Lift the courgettes from the oil, drain and place on kitchen paper to absorb the excess oil. Repeat with the remaining courgettes and season well before serving.

Here are two indispensable side dishes of the root vegetables that are so plentiful in autumn and winter months. If you are using large old carrots, they have had a lot of time to develop their natural sugars, says John. Small carrots, on the other hand, may require a teaspoon of sugar to help them. Boiling the parsnips before frying helps to ensure that these notoriously woody vegetables are perfectly tender – but don't boil them too long.

glazed carrots

Serves 4
5 large carrots
salt and pepper
80ml chicken stock
20g butter

Peel the carrots and cut them into batons about 6cm long and 1cm square.

Bring a saucepan of salted water to the boil and add the carrots. Cook in rapidly boiling water for 4 minutes or until tender.

Drain the carrots and place them in a large flat pan like a deep-sided frying pan. Add the chicken stock and butter. Bring to the boil and reduce over a medium heat until there is very little liquid left in the pan and the carrots take on a shiny, glazed appearance.

Season and serve immediately.

honey parsnips

Serves 4
5 large parsnips
salt and pepper
3 thyme sprigs
iced water
 2 tbsp vegetable oil
30g honey

Peel the parsnips and cut them in half lengthways. Slice each half into batons and remove the core.

Bring a saucepan of salted water to the boil and add the parsnips. Cook them in rapidly boiling water for 3 minutes or until tender.

Meanwhile, chop the thyme finely.

Drain the parsnips then refresh them in a bowl of iced water. Drain again and dry thoroughly in a clean kitchen cloth.

Heat the oil in a heavy-based frying pan. Season the parsnips with salt and pepper and, when the oil is hot, brown the parsnips on all sides.

Add the honey to the pan and allow it to gently caramelise. Sprinkle in the thyme, season to taste and serve immediately.

Peas and bacon is a marriage that works very well, says Angela of this classic way of jazzing up everyone's favourite green vegetable. However, if you have vegetarians to cater for you could simply leave out the bacon. The surprise, for many, is the inclusion of lettuce in a warm dish. Angela likes serving this with roasts, or with sautéed scallops, and while frozen peas are acceptable, she does recommend you aim to use fresh peas in season.

peas *à la française*

Serves 4
20 baby onions
100g butter
salt and pepper
150g pancetta lardons
500g fresh peas
2 baby gem lettuces, thinly sliced

Peel the onions, leaving them whole. Heat half the butter in a frying pan, add the onions and cook over a low-to-moderate heat, stirring frequently, until soft and golden. Season well with salt and pepper.

Meanwhile, in a separate frying pan, sauté the lardons until golden brown.

Cook the peas in a pan of boiling salted water for 5 minutes. Drain all the water from the peas and return them to the saucepan.

Add most of the remaining butter, the onions and lardons and mix well.

Stir in the thinly sliced baby gem, season to taste, dot with the last of the butter and serve.

There is little point making this traditional warming favourite when cauliflower is not in season, says Angela. It is also important that the cauliflower is properly tender, otherwise the result will be disappointing. Buy the best cheddar you can afford to give a lovely cheesy flavour.

cauliflower cheese

Serves 4

1 cauliflower
salt and pepper
40g butter
40g flour
400-500ml milk
grated nutmeg
150g cheddar cheese, grated, plus
  extra for sprinkling

Separate the cauliflower into florets, discarding the core and leaves.

Put the cauliflower in a saucepan, cover with salted water and bring to the boil. Cook for 5-8 minutes, until tender to the point of a knife.

Meanwhile, melt the butter in a separate saucepan over a low-to-moderate heat. Add the flour and stir to make a paste. Cook for about 5 minutes, stirring from time to time.

Pour one-third of the milk to the pan and whisk until well blended. Stir in the rest of the milk and add some salt, pepper and a few gratings of nutmeg.

Cook over a medium heat for 15 minutes.

When the cauliflower is cooked, drain it thoroughly and allow it to dry.

Add the grated cheese to the sauce and mix well, then stir in the cauliflower.

Preheat the grill. Pour the cauliflower cheese mixture into a heatproof serving dish. Sprinkle with the extra grated cheddar and grill until the cheese has melted and the top is golden brown.

A nourishing alternative to baked beans, this hearty dish is the Tuscan equivalent of cassoulet, says Angela. You can serve it as is, or alongside some grilled Italian sausages, or a roast leg of lamb. Alternatively, leave it to cool then add some red wine vinaigrette, and maybe some grain mustard, to transform it into a salad. Almost any dried bean will do here, so feel free to try borlotti, kidney, haricot blanc, flageolet, cacao beans and others.

tuscan beans

250g dried cannellini beans
250g dried other type of bean (see above)
2 x 75g pieces pancetta
1 onion
2 small carrots
2 celery sticks, strings removed
a little olive oil
2 garlic cloves
1 bay leaf
4 thyme sprigs

Soak both varieties of bean, separately, overnight in bowls of cold water.

Next day, drain the beans, which should have plumped up.

Cut the onion, carrots and celery into even-sized largish pieces.

Heat a casserole or large saucepan with a little olive oil. Add half the vegetables, one piece of the pancetta and one garlic clove, and cook until the vegetables are lightly coloured.

Add the cannellini beans to the pan and cover with water. Add half the herbs. Bring to the boil and cook over a low heat, adding more water if necessary, until the beans are tender.

Repeat this process in another saucepan with the remaining vegetables, pancetta, beans and herbs.

When the beans are cooked, season to taste with salt and pepper. Mix the contents of both pans together, discarding any excess cooking liquid, and serve.

Currently very fashionable in restaurants, purées are, says Angela, a great way of incorporating vegetables into a dish. It is important to use the ripest, most colourful varieties you can and to cook them thoroughly so that the texture is in no way grainy. Potato and cauliflower can both be substituted for the root vegetables featured here, and basil can be used in place of parsley.

vegetable purées

1 large celeriac or 4 large carrots
50g butter, plus a few cubes cold butter extra
salt and pepper
about 100ml light vegetable stock

Peel the celeriac, discarding the knobbly bits at the bottom, and cut into rough dice. If using carrots, peel them and cut into rough dice.

Melt the butter in a saucepan, add the celeriac or carrot and sweat over a low-medium heat until soft but not coloured.

Add some salt, then pour in the stock and continue cooking until the vegetable is very soft.

Use a stick blender to blitz the mixture to a purée. If necessary to get a really smooth and shiny purée, add a few cubes of cold butter and extra stock.

Season the purée to taste with salt and pepper then pass it through a chinois. If necessary, reheat it gently to serve.

Variation To make parsley purée, pick all the leaves from a large bunch of parsley and cook them in a pan of boiling salted water until soft. Drain well then put the parsley in a liquidiser. Purée, adding some salt and pepper and 50g butter towards the end to add taste and shine. Pass the mixture through a chinois straight into a mixing bowl set over ice to cool the purée as quickly as possible and keep its colour. This is especially good with turkey at Christmas.

Artichokes are a variety of thistle which makes a stunning garden plant but have spiky forms of natural protection that need to be removed to reach the tender heart. Here is Angela's method of preparing them ready for cooking.

preparing artichokes

✳✳

artichokes
1 lemon, sliced
dash of vinegar or lemon juice

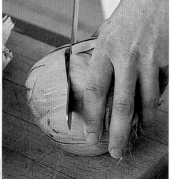

Use a vegetable peeler to peel the thick skin from the base of the choke as well as down the stalk, so that the whitish flesh underneath is showing.

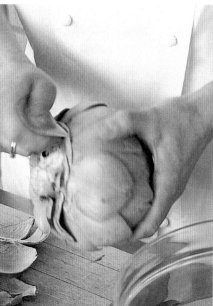

Discard the outer leaves of each artichoke.

Cut off the leaves just where the choke starts, about two-thirds of the way up the leaves. Trim off the base.

Use a spoon to scoop out all the hairs and tiny leaves left in the choke.

Peel off the leaves around the heart.

Rub the artichokes with lemon and drop them immediately into a bowl of acidulated water to prevent discoloration.

To cook the artichoke hearts, braise them in a saucepan of water adding a dash of white wine vinegar, lemon juice, olive oil, a few coriander seeds, thyme sprigs and a garlic clove. Bring to the boil and cook them until they are just tender when pierced with a sharp knife. leave them to cool in the liquid and store them in that liquid in the fridge. If the artichokes are particularly large, you could cut them into quarters or eighths before cooking.

Angela is passionate about this vegetarian dish, which can also be served as a main course accompaniment to lamb, as a hot starter, or cold for lunch. Make up a batch or two and store them in the freezer, ready to defrost as needed. It can be oily, so tip off any excess when it comes out of the oven.

aubergine parmigiana

6 large aubergines

about 100ml olive oil

200ml fresh tomato sauce with herbs and garlic

salt and pepper

200g buffalo mozzarella

½ bunch basil

150g grated parmesan

Tip

For the best result, try to slice the aubergines as thinly as possible and keep the individual layers thin as you build the dish.

Cut the unpeeled aubergines into slices about 5-12mm thick (a mandolin slicer is good for this).

Heat some of the olive oil in a frying pan over a medium heat. Working in batches, fry each slice of aubergine on both sides until lightly coloured. You will have to add more oil for each batch as the aubergine drinks it up, but try to use as little as you can get away with, or the finished dish will be too oily. Lay the cooked slices on kitchen paper to absorb any excess oil.

Heat the tomato sauce in a small pan. Taste and add some salt and pepper if necessary.

Cut the mozzarella into small dice. Pick the leaves from the basil sprigs and shred them finely.

Preheat the oven to 180°C/gas 4.

The ingredients need to be layered in an ovenproof dish ready for baking. Start with about a quarter of the tomato sauce, spreading it out in the dish. Add a layer of about one-third of the aubergines, overlapping, then another quarter of the tomato sauce. Cover that with half the diced mozzarella, one-third of the parmesan and half the basil.

Top with a second layer of aubergine and continue repeating the layers, finishing with another layer of aubergine. Sprinkle with the last of the parmesan.

Cover the dish with foil and bake for 20 minutes, by which time the aubergine should be hot in the centre and the sauce bubbling up at the sides.

Discard the foil. Use a spoon to press down at the sides of the dish as these cook faster and thus tend to rise and colour more rapidly. Bake for a further 5 minutes, until the parmesan colours.

9 desserts

At John's base in Devon, in south-west England, there are plenty of plum varieties grown locally. His particular favourite for this dish is the Dittisham plum, but you could use any variety, from dark pungent damsons to pink-blushed Victorias or greengages. The peppery flavour of the sticky ginger adds another dimension to the flavour and helps cut the sweetness.

poached plums *with ginger cream*

Serves 4
400g plums
110g sugar
1 cinnamon stick
250ml cream
2 tsp icing sugar
1 tsp ground ginger
½ piece preserved ginger

Halve the plums and carefully remove the stones.

Put 150ml water in a saucepan with the sugar and cinnamon stick and bring to the boil. Skim the surface of any froth.

Reduce the heat, add the plums to the syrup and poach gently until they are soft but not mushy. Set aside to cool. Reserve the cinnamon stick for decoration if you like.

Combine the cream, icing sugar and ground ginger in a large bowl and whip until the cream forms soft peaks. Finely chop the preserved ginger and fold it into the cream.

Serve the plums with a generous spoonful of ginger cream on top and decorate with pieces of cinnamon stick if you like.

This dish evokes memories of childhood for Angela. It can be made with eating apples but cooking varieties give the best result. She recommends leaving the apples to stand for two or three hours before baking so that the apples have time to absorb the flavours of the stuffing. They will be really very hot when removed from the oven, so let them to stand for ten minutes or so before serving. Alternatively, try serving the baked apples cold.

baked apples

Serves 4

50g sultanas

50g raisins

50g walnuts, chopped

dash of calvados

100g sugar

4 cooking apples

100g butter, diced

double cream, for serving

Tip

If you have no calvados, in the house, simply choose another liqueur, or else use plain water.

In a bowl, mix the dried fruit and nuts with the calvados and half the sugar. Leave the fruit to absorb the alcohol.

When ready to cook, preheat the oven to 180°C/gas 4. Core the apples and place them in an ovenproof dish. Fill the holes with the fruit mixture.

Cover the apples with the diced butter and sprinkle with the remaining sugar. Pour 100ml water into the dish and cover with foil.

Bake for 30-40 minutes until soft, removing the foil halfway through cooking. The apples should be soft but not so much that they loose their shape.

Remove the dish from the oven and serve the apples with the double cream.

Kids love this dish, says John, and it is a great way to encourage them to eat fruit. He favours the lovely Williams variety of pear for it, because it is so succulent, but any high-quality dessert pear will do. Save your woody Conference pears for making chutneys and pies.

poached pears *with chocolate sauce*

Serves 4
120g caster sugar
175ml dessert wine
juice of 1 lemon
4 pears
icing sugar, for dusting

For the chocolate sauce
110g dark chocolate
75ml cream

In a pan, combine the caster sugar, dessert wine, lemon juice and 270ml water. Bring to the boil.

Meanwhile, peel the pears but leave them whole. Skim the froth from the surface of the syrup and then carefully add the pears.

Gently poach the pears until they are soft, but not mushy. Take off the heat and allow to cool.

Make the chocolate sauce: break the chocolate up, put it in a heatproof bowl and place the bowl over a pan of lightly simmering water. Stir continuously until all the chocolate has melted.

Slowly stir the cream into the chocolate. Take the bowl off the heat and keep to one side.

Place one pear per person on the serving plates and drizzle the chocolate sauce around. Dust with icing sugar and serve immediately.

John loves fresh figs and advises the best ones for this dish, which can be served hot or cold, are the large purple-tinged varieties, not small green ones. Combining them with port and caramelised almond flakes helps cut the natural richness of the fruit. The sugar syrup used as an ingredient in this dish will come in handy for several other desserts in this book.

baked figs *in port*

Serves 4
8 purple figs
4 tbsp port
50g unsalted butter
1 vanilla pod, split in half
freshly ground black pepper
2 tsp honey
110g flaked almonds
icing sugar, for dusting
crème fraîche, to serve

For the sugar syrup
50g caster sugar

Tip
The leftover sugar syrup will keep in the fridge for around five days. Use it for poaching other fruits and rhubarb, adding herb and spice flavours as desired, or for chocolate mousse.

First make some sugar syrup. Stir the caster sugar and 100ml water in a saucepan over a low heat until the sugar has dissolved. Then raise the heat under the pan and bring the syrup to a boil. Simmer for 1 minute, then remove the pan from the heat.

Preheat the oven to 240°C/gas 9. Prick the figs all over using a fork.

Gently heat the port in a casserole and allow to bubble until it has reduced by half. Add the butter, 6 tablespoons of the sugar syrup, the vanilla pod and a generous grinding of black pepper.

Bring to the boil, then gently add the figs and the honey.

Transfer to the oven for 5-6 minutes, basting the figs occasionally.

Meanwhile, sprinkle the flaked almonds on to a non-stick baking tray and dust generously with icing sugar. Bake in the oven for a few minutes, until golden brown.

To serve, arrange the figs on serving plates and drizzle the poaching liquid over them. Scatter with the caramelised almonds and decorate with the vanilla if you like. Serve with a dollop of crème fraîche.

Sometimes the best conclusion to a meal is a few mouthfuls of light tangy, fruit-flavoured cream, and – even better – these old English recipes can be prepared a day ahead of serving. For a fancier presentation, Angela suggests jelly or melon and mint salad as accompaniments to the posset, while John recommends a shortbread or tuile biscuit for the fool.

lemon posset

Serves 4
1/4 gelatine leaf
500ml double cream
125g sugar
juice of 3 lemons

Soak the piece of gelatine leaf in a bowl of iced water for 5 minutes or until soft.

Put the cream and sugar in a saucepan, bring to the boil and simmer for 3-4 minutes.

Add the lemon juice to the cream and boil for another 3-4 minutes.

Remove the pan from the heat. Squeeze the excess water from the now-spongy gelatine and stir it into the cream until it has completely dissolved.

Pass the cream mixture through a fine sieve and into a jug, then pour it into individual serving glasses. Leave to set in the fridge overnight.

gooseberry fool

Serves 4
300g gooseberries, topped and tailed
90g unsalted butter
110g caster sugar
4 egg yolks plus 1 whole egg
200ml whipping cream

Tip
Gooseberries have a tendency to stick and burn, so it's best to cook them slowly.

Put the gooseberries and butter in a heavy-based saucepan over a very low heat and cook until the fruit is very soft.

Push the gooseberries through a fine sieve to make a purée, trapping the seeds in the sieve (you can discard them).

Put the purée in a saucepan with the sugar, egg yolks and whole egg. Again on a low heat, cook the purée until it thickens. Do not let the mixture boil, otherwise the eggs will scramble.

When the mixture has thickened, pour it into a bowl or tray and allow to cool, then chill. Ideally it should be fridge cold.

Whip the cream until it forms soft peaks and gently fold it into the purée. Spoon the fool into serving glasses and chill before eating.

This foamy Italian sauce-cum-dessert is amazing, says Angela. It is traditionally made with Marsala wine, a rich fortified wine from Sicily, but she happily splashes in whisky, brandy, dry white wine or port instead. Zabaglione can can be served hot, warm, or left to set in glasses overnight and served cold the next day, perhaps with some warm roast fruit, or simply with almond-flavoured amaretti biscuits.

zabaglione *with crushed amaretti*

Serves 4
12 amaretti biscuits
8 egg yolks
200g sugar
200ml marsala or sweet dessert wine
50ml whisky
50ml brandy

Put the amaretti in a bowl and crush them with the end of a rolling pin. Divide between four serving glasses and set aside.

Half-fill a saucepan with water and bring it to the boil.

Meanwhile, take a large heatproof bowl that will sit over the saucepan without the base touching the water. Put the egg yolks and sugar in it and whisk until the mixture is creamy and light in colour. Add the marsala or sweet wine, whisky and brandy and whisk again.

Set the bowl over the pan of simmering water and continue whisking for 5-8 minutes. Once the whisk leaves a pattern in the surface of the mixture, it is ready.

Pour the hot zabaglione over the amaretti and serve.

If preferred, you can layer this popular Italian dessert in individual serving glasses rather than one large dish. Angela says tiramisu usually tastes better the day after making, because the sponge fingers have had time to absorb the coffee and alcohol flavourings. Mascarpone is often called cheese but in fact it is a cultured cream. Angela recommends buying the best quality you can afford for a superior result.

tiramisu

Serves 4-6
100ml strong brewed espresso coffee
50ml Kahlúa liqueur
50ml amaretto
chocolate shavings, to decorate

For the sponge fingers
6 eggs, separated
170g sugar
few drops of lemon juice
85g cornflour
115g plain flour, sifted

For the mousse
4 eggs, separated
150g caster sugar
450g mascarpone, at room temperature
190ml double cream

To make the sponge fingers, preheat the oven to 180°C/gas 4 and line a baking tray with parchment paper.

Whisk the egg yolks with one-third of the sugar until the mixture is light and creamy.

In a separate large bowl, whisk the egg whites with one-third of the sugar and the lemon juice until the whites have trebled in volume. Gradually add the cornflour and the remaining sugar, whisking after each addition.

Fold the meringue into the yolk mixture, then fold in the sifted flour. Pour the batter over the lined baking sheet, spreading it out to a depth of 1-1.5cm. Smooth over the surface and bake in the oven for 10-15 minutes until golden.

To make the mousse, in a mixing bowl, whisk the egg yolks with 30g caster sugar until the mixture is very pale and creamy. Fold the mascarpone into the yolks.

In a separate large bowl, whisk the egg whites with 120g sugar until stiff peaks form when the whisk is lifted from the whites. Fold the yolk mixture and the meringue together.

Whip the cream until it forms soft peaks when the whisk is lifted from the bowl. Fold the cream into the egg mixture and set aside.

Mix the coffee, Kahlúa and amaretto together. Cut the baked sponge into fingers and soak them in the coffee mixture.

Spoon a layer of mousse mixture into a large serving bowl. Cover with a layer of coffee-soaked sponge fingers. Continue alternating the layers until the ingredients have all been used, finishing with a layer of mousse.

Chill the tiramisu for at least 2 hours before serving. Sprinkle the surface with chocolate shavings before taking it to the table.

Homemade granita and sorbet are wonderful ways of using up gluts of seasonal fruit and preserving them for enjoyment through the rest of the year, says Angela. Granita never freezes solid because of its high alcohol content and has a pretty granular texture reminiscent of slushie drinks. Sorbet, on the other hand, sets smoothly and has a higher fruit content.

whisky granita

Serves 4
150g caster sugar
100ml whisky

In a saucepan, combine the caster sugar and 500ml water, and place over a low heat. Stir until the sugar has dissolved, then bring the syrup to the boil and remove from the heat.

Meanwhile, fill a mixing bowl with ice cubes. Put the hot syrup in another bowl (preferably metal) and place it over the bowl of ice to help it cool and chill quickly.

When the syrup is cold, stir in the whisky. Pour the mixture into plastic or metal trays or other containers and leave to freeze overnight.

Just before serving, remove the trays from the freezer and break up the mixture with a fork to create tiny shards of ice. Serve immediately.

passion fruit & vodka sorbet

Serves 4
150g sugar
200g passion fruit purée
100ml vodka

In a saucepan, combine the caster sugar and 350ml water, and place over a low heat. Stir until the sugar has dissolved, then bring the syrup to the boil and remove from the heat.

Meanwhile, fill a mixing bowl with ice cubes. Put the hot syrup in another bowl (preferably metal) and place it over the bowl of ice to help it cool and chill quickly.

When the syrup is cold, stir in the passion fruit purée and vodka. Churn in an ice cream machine, following the manufacturer's instructions, to make a sorbet, or follow the instructions above to make granita.

other iced delights

When you're having friends over for a meal, chill out with an ice cream, sorbet or granita – they are all made well in advance of serving, leaving you calm and organised when it is time to dish up dessert. As the variations here show, they can be as simple or luxurious as you please.

Orange granita

This is even easier to make than the whisky version on page 212. Mix 850ml orange juice with 100ml Grand Marnier and the finely grated zest of one orange. Pour into a tray and freeze overnight. The alcohol prevents it freezing solid, so all you need to do next day is break it up with a fork to create shards of ice.

Try a coffee granita

Coffee granita is great served with a brownie, well-flavoured chocolate cake, mousse or tiramisu (try it with the recipes on page 244 and 211). When making it, be sure to use a good-quality, freshly brewed espresso or other strong coffee and try alcohols such as aniseed-flavoured sambuca, chocolatey Tia Maria, grappa or brandy. You will need about 2 tablespoons of alcohol for 500ml coffee and 150g caster sugar. Once you've forked it up, serve the granita in chilled coffee cups with a dash of whipped cream, if you like.

Other creamy bases

For some restaurant sophistication, try fromage frais sorbet flavoured with black pepper. First make a stock syrup: dissolve 100g caster sugar in 120ml water and bring to the boil. Leave to cool, then stir in 200g chilled fromage frais and ¼ teaspoon freshly ground black pepper. Churn in an ice cream machine following the manufacturer's instructions, then put the sorbet in the freezer for at least 6 hours before serving, so that the pepper flavour has time to develop.

You can also make ices with ingredients such as sweetened greek yoghurt and mascarpone. With the latter, do not churn too much, or the texture will be like butter. On the final few turns of the machine, you can add a handful of chopped roasted nuts or chocolate pieces for flavour and crunch.

How about a cocktail?

Granita has the correct texture when it is icy but melts as soon as it hits the mouth. This makes it terrific for mixing in cocktails as well as serving as a refreshing summer dessert.

Mint and choc-chip ice cream

For this classic Italian gelateria favourite, make a custard base with 500ml milk, 6 egg yolks and 125g caster sugar. Fold in 250ml whipped double cream and 1 tablespoon mint essence, then churn, adding 200g choc chip pieces in the final stages.

Pistachio ice cream

This is wonderful served with chocolate desserts. To make it, follow the basic recipe for almond ice cream on the left, using a spoonful of canned pistachio paste instead of ground almonds, and omit the marzipan and amandine liqueur. Even though you are using a paste you still need to pass the mixture through a fine sieve to ensure the ice cream has a smooth texture.

Dress up your ice creams and sorbets

Try garnishes such as chopped roasted nuts, grated bitter chocolate (great with vanilla ice cream), and warm fruit compotes or poached fruits. Or why not revert to childhood and enjoy them sandwiched between crisp wafers? Let the ice cream soften in the fridge so that it's just malleable. Sandwich scoops of it between wafers and freeze until firm.

Almond ice cream

As featured in the peach gratin on page 234. Bring 150ml of milk to boiling point in a saucepan, then add 15g ground almonds and leave to infuse for 10 minutes off the heat. In a mixing bowl, whisk 3 egg yolks and 50g caster sugar together and set aside.

Strain the milk through a fine sieve, pressing down well on the almonds. Add 150ml cream and crumble in 15g marzipan. Return the milk to the heat and bring to boiling point. Pour the mixture on to the egg yolks, whisking continuously, then pour the custard back into the saucepan and cook gently until the custard coats the back of a spoon.

Strain the custard into a clean bowl and add 2 tablespoons amandine liqueur. Allow to cool and chill before churning the mixture in an ice cream machine.

No ice cream machine?

You get the best texture using a machine to churn sorbets and ice cream. If you don't have one, there is another method. Pour the mixture into a wide plastic or metal box and freeze for about 90 minutes, until icy at the edges. Transfer to a food processor and whiz until slushy, or beat thoroughly with an electric whisk. Return to the freezer and continue freezing for another 90 minutes. Repeat the whisking and freezing processes two or three times until the mixture has a good texture.

Angela's beautiful jellied dessert of fresh citrus fruits and berries – a fancy take on simple fruit and cream – is best served at the height of summer when the berries are at their most ripe. If you would like to experiment, try using this recipe as a base for a trifle.

blood orange jelly

Serves 4
2 leaves gelatine
300ml blood orange juice
50g sugar
4 oranges
2 grapefruit
1 punnet strawberries
1 punnet raspberries

Tip

Many chefs prefer leaf to powdered gelatine as the former gives a clearer finish to the jelly.

Put the gelatine in a bowl of cold water and leave it to soak until the gelatine has turned spongy.

Meanwhile, bring the orange juice and sugar to the boil in a small saucepan. Remove the pan from the heat. Squeeze the excess water from the spongy gelatine and add it to the pan, stirring to dissolve. Set aside to cool.

Segment the oranges and grapefruit, following the instructions on page 62. Cut the strawberries in half and finely shred the mint leaves. Add them to the orange and grapefruit segments and mix gently.

Spoon the fruit into serving bowls, then cover with the gelatine mixture, dividing it evenly among the dishes. Place in the fridge to set for at least 2 hours.

Variation For a dinner party top the jelly with chantilly cream and serve with some nice biscuits.

If you can make a pancake batter, you can make clafoutis, says John. It is like a sweet Yorkshire pudding studded with fruit and very quick to make. This delightful dessert comes from the Limousin region of France which produces superb cherries. For a pleasant change, try it with blueberries.

cherry & almond *clafoutis*

Serves 4

220g fresh cherries, washed

butter, for greasing

200ml whole milk

30g marzipan

2 whole eggs, plus 1 extra egg yolk

50g caster sugar

30ml amaretto

15g plain flour

icing sugar

Tip
Traditionally the stones are left in the cherries for this dish to give more flavour, but you could pit them first if preferred. Use a cherry stoning gadget, or else cut them in half and lift the pits out with a sharp pointed knife.

Preheat the oven to 160°C/gas 3.

Take an ovenproof dish large enough to hold the cherries in one layer. Grease it with butter and put the cherries in it. (When serving, do remember to tell people that the cherries still have their stones.)

Warm half the milk in a saucepan. Whisk in the marzipan, allowing it to melt.

In a mixing bowl, whisk together the eggs, egg yolk, caster sugar and the remaining milk.

Strain the warm milk from the saucepan into the egg mixture, then add the amaretto.

Sieve the flour into the bowl then whisk to form a smooth batter. Sieve the batter over the cherries.

Bake the clafoutis for 20-30 minutes, until set, then remove from the oven and set aside to cool. Dust with icing sugar and serve warm.

Here John revisits Britain's traditional crumble. The result is lighter, as it contains no flour, yet deliciously nutty and undeniably glamorous when served with a fresh sauce of strawberries, lime and crème de fraise, the French strawberry liqueur. It is a great way to show off the bright pink stalks of new-season's forced rhubarb, says John.

rhubarb crumble *with strawberry sauce*

Serves 2

20ml sugar syrup (see page 207)

8 x 7cm batons thick pink (forced) rhubarb

50ml whipping cream

clotted cream

For the crumble topping

50g walnuts

2 tsp caster sugar

½ tsp cinnamon

30g butter

For the strawberry sauce

150g strawberries, washed and hulled

50g icing sugar

juice of 1 lime

20ml crème de fraise

Preheat the oven to 220°C/ gas 7.

Heat the sugar syrup in a saucepan. Add the rhubarb and cook over a high heat until the syrup has reduced by half and glazes the fruit. Set aside in an ovenproof dish.

Make the crumble topping: In a food processor, blitz the walnuts, caster sugar and cinnamon together, keeping the mixture a little coarse. Add the butter and process for 10-20 seconds more.

Sprinkle the walnut mixture over the rhubarb and bake in the oven for 10 minutes.

Meanwhile, make the sauce: put the strawberries in a liquidiser with the icing sugar, lime juice and crème de fraise, and blend until smooth. Taste and add more sugar if desired.

Whip the whipping cream lightly until frothy.

When the crumble is done, use a spatula to transfer it to the centre of your serving plates. Spoon around the strawberry sauce and decorate with splashes of the frothy cream. Top with a spoonful of clotted cream and serve.

While this looks elegantly fragile, this dessert is fairly easy to prepare and offers the convenience of advance preparation, says Angela. It is essentially raspberries and cream served with shortbread biscuits, but cleverly layered for a spectacular presentation – and you don't have to do the full three layers if you don't want to. Angela says its great served for afternoon tea. Try substituting blackberries or sliced nectarines for the raspberries.

raspberry shortcake

Serves 4-6

For the shortcake pastry
150g unsalted butter, diced
250g plain flour
small pinch salt
80g caster sugar
1 egg, plus 1 extra egg yolk

For the filling
200ml double cream
*55g icing sugar, sieved, plus extra for
  dusting*
½ vanilla pod, split
2 punnets raspberries

Preheat the oven to 160°C/gas 4. Line two or three baking trays with greaseproof paper.

To make the pastry, combine the butter, flour and salt in a large bowl and rub together until the mixture resembles fine breadcrumbs. Stir in the sugar.

Beat the whole eggs and yolks together in a jug. Add just enough egg to the flour mixture to make smooth dough, being careful not to overwork it. Bring the dough together into a ball and gently flatten. Wrap in cling film and chill for up to 30 minutes.

Roll out the pastry on a lightly floured surface to a thickness of about 5mm. Cut out 12 x 8cm rounds using a cutter or small plate as a template. Place the pastry discs on the lined baking trays and bake for 5-8 minutes, or until golden brown. Remove the pastry from the oven and set aside to cool.

Meanwhile, combine the double cream and icing sugar in a mixing bowl. Split the vanilla pod and scrape the seeds into the cream. Whip the cream until it forms soft peaks when the whisk is lifted from the bowl. Chill until required.

When almost ready to serve, spoon a little of the sweetened cream into the centre of a plate. Setting aside the best looking pastry disc to present on top of the shortcake, place one pastry disc on top of the cream. Arrange a layer of raspberries over this. Spoon the cream mixture over the fruit and repeat the layers, finishing with the best looking pastry disc.

Dust with icing sugar and take the raspberry shortcake to the table.

Unlike many people, Angela does not believe that the whole point of carrot cake is the American-style cream cheese frosting! If you do want to ice it, though, she recommends classic butter icing, or a layer of whipped mascarpone sweetened with icing sugar. Some people are surprised by the high amount of vegetable oil in the batter but, says Angela, it is an important part of the dish and keeps it moist during the long, slow baking process. The cake should keep for three or four days after baking.

carrot cake

Serves 8

butter for the tin

flour for the tin

2 large eggs

170g sugar

150ml vegetable oil

200g wholemeal flour

3 tsp mixed spice

1 tsp bicarbonate soda

200g carrot, grated

110g sultanas

50g walnuts

50g pine nuts

icing sugar, to serve (optional)

whipped mascarpone or cream, to
   serve (optional)

Grease a 14cm round cake tin with butter and dust the inside with flour, tapping it around to ensure it is evenly coated.

In a large mixing bow, beat the eggs, sugar and oil together. Mix in the wholemeal flour, mixed spice and bicarbonate of soda to create a batter.

Fold in the grated carrot, sultanas, walnuts and pine nuts until evenly distributed.

Pour the mixture into the prepared cake tin, being careful not to fill it more than two-thirds full as the mixture will rise when baked.

Bake for 1 hour or until well risen. To test if it is done, insert a skewer in the centre of the cake, then remove it - if it is clean, the cake is ready, if not continue baking for a few more minutes and test again.

Keep in an airtight tin for three or four days before serving, dusted with icing sugar, cut in wedges and accompanied by whipped mascarpone or cream if you like.

The green lemony flavour of cardamom adds a subtle sweetness to John's little baked custards that will have your guests guessing. A good crème caramel should slip and slither delicately down the throat, he says, so be sure to remove all foam from the custard before baking.

cardamom crème caramel

Serves 5
100g sugar
5 cardamom pods
500ml milk
3 whole eggs

Preheat the oven to 150°C/gas 2.

Measure out 50g of the sugar and place it in a heavy-based saucepan. Moisten it with a little water, taking care not to add too much.

Put the pan over a medium heat and stir until the sugar has dissolved. Bring to the boil and cook rapidly until it colours to a light caramel.

Remove the pan from the heat and add a tablespoon of water - take care, as it will splutter.

Swirl the pan around to mix the water and caramel together, then pour a little into the base of five dariole moulds. The texture should be like a soft eating caramel, not like hard toffee.

Crush the cardamom pods with a rolling pin and put them in a clean saucepan with the milk. Bring to the boil then remove from the heat and allow it to cool just a little.

Carefully pass the milk through a fine sieve to remove the cardamom.

Combine the eggs and remaining caster sugar in a large bowl and mix well. Whisk the hot milk into the egg mixture to make a custard.

Pour the custard into the prepared moulds, almost filling them. Put the moulds in a baking tray and half-fill the tray with water.

Put the tray of custards in the oven to poach for 30-40 minutes, or until set. Do not let the water in the tray come to the boil.

Remove the custards from the oven and allow to cool.

When ready to serve, run a pointed knife around the inside of each mould, turn over on to a plate and carefully shake the custard out.

You don't want the filling for this tart to taste too eggy, says Angela, so be sure to use plenty of vanilla and nutmeg. For the perfect texture, have the confidence to take it out of the oven before the filling is firm and leave it to cool to room temperature (not in the refrigerator).

vanilla custard tart

Serves 8-10

½ recipe quantity Rich sweet pastry
(pages 30-33)

flour, for dusting

1 egg, beaten

For the filling

600ml single cream

1 vanilla pod, split and scraped

freshly grated nutmeg to taste

50g caster sugar

3 large whole eggs, plus 2 large
yolks

Preheat the oven to 180°C/gas 4. Roll the pastry out thinly and use it to line a 30cm tart pan.

Line the pastry case with greaseproof paper, then fill it with baking beans or rice. Bake for 15-20 minutes until the pastry is just beginning to turn golden brown at the edges, removing the beans and paper about two-thirds of the way through.

Remove the pastry case from the oven and brush it all over the inside with the egg wash. Return to the oven and bake for another 5 minutes, until the egg is cooked. Repeat the brushing and baking process twice more, to ensure the base of the pastry case is completely sealed.

To make the filling, bring the cream, vanilla pod and seeds, and grated nutmeg to taste to the boil in a saucepan.

In a large mixing bowl, whisk the sugar, whole eggs and yolks together.

When the cream has reached boiling point, spoon out and discard the vanilla pod, then pour the cream over the eggs, whisking constantly.

Lower the oven setting to 170°C/gas 3. Pour the custard filling into the tart case and bake for 30-40 minutes, until the filling is firm in the centre.

This is a simple old-fashioned lemon tart with passion fruit added for a crunchy texture and slightly spicy flavour, says John. Try to find purple wrinkled passion fruit, rather than the smooth-skinned pale varieties, as they produce more juice and have a stronger flavour.

lemon & passion fruit *flan*

Serves 8-10

400g sweet pastry (see pages 30-33)

butter, for greasing

2 lemons

175g caster sugar

4 whole eggs

150ml double cream

2 passion fruit

Roll out the ball of pastry into a circle approximately 32cm in diameter. Take a 28cm flan tin with a removable base and grease it with butter.

Pick up the pastry by rolling it over the rolling pin, then unroll it over the prepared tin, making sure it is centred. Lift up the edges of the pastry and push the pastry into the corners of the tin. Pinch upwards all the way around the tin to trim the edges. Prick the base all over with a fork and put the pastry case in the refrigerator to chill for 30 minutes.

Preheat the oven to 200°C/gas 6. Cover the pastry case with greaseproof paper and baking beans, and bake for 15-20 minutes, or until golden brown and crisp, removing the paper and beans halfway through cooking.

Meanwhile, make the filling. Finely grate the zest from the lemons and squeeze the juice. Combine them in a mixing bowl with the sugar and eggs and whisk together well. Whisk in the cream.

Pass the custard through a sieve into a clean bowl. Scoop out the flesh and juice of the passion fruit and add to the custard, stirring well.

Carefully check the pastry case for any holes or cracks - otherwise the filling may leak out during cooking. Fill any gaps with a little of the raw pastry trimmings, softened between your thumb and forefinger.

Set the oven temperature to 180°C/gas 4. Put the empty pastry case on the oven shelf and pour in the lemon custard, making sure the passion fruit seeds are evenly distributed.

Bake for 30-40 minutes, or until the custard is just cooked: it should wobble when the flan case is tapped.

Remove the tart from the oven and leave it to cool on a wire rack. Ideally it should be eaten at room temperature, not cold.

There are so many potential variations for this delicious tart, says Angela, so make the most of whatever is in season and swap the plums for apricots, peaches or nectarines. Shape it into individual tartlets if you prefer, and serve warm or cold. The sweet pastry and frangipane can be made well in advance and stored in practical batches in the freezer, ready for quickly assembling tarts on other occasions. Once baked, this tart can happily be stored for two to three days in an airtight container.

plum & almond tart

Serves 6-8

1 recipe quantity rich sweet pastry
(pages 30-33)

flour, for dusting

5-6 ripe plums, cut into eighths,
stones removed

icing sugar, for dusting

whipped cream or crème fraîche, to
serve

For the frangipane

200g unsalted butter

200g caster sugar

2 eggs

200g ground almonds

To make the frangipane, beat the butter and sugar together in a bowl until light and creamy. Add the eggs one at a time, beating well after each addition. Add the ground almonds and mix well. Set aside.

Preheat the oven to 180°C/gas 4. Roll the rich sweet pastry out thinly and use it to line a large tart ring or 6-8 individual tartlet rings about 8cm diameter.

Spoon the frangipane into the tart case so that it comes about halfway up the side and smooth over the surface. Cover the frangipane evenly with the fruit.

Bake for 30-40 minutes (15-25 minutes for the tartlets) until the pastry is crisp and golden brown and the fruit is tender.

Remove the tart from the oven. Dust with icing sugar and serve warm with whipped cream or crème fraîche.

John's show-stopping fruit pudding is a wonderfully light and succulent dessert to serve when peaches are in season. In France this type of dish is referred to as chaud-froid, because it is both hot and cold, the heat of the grilled fruit and sabayon sauce contrasting with the chill of the almond ice cream. Use apricots or nectarines in place of the peaches if they are in better condition. Instead of finishing the dish under the grill, you could brown it carefully with a cook's blowtorch.

peach *gratin*

Serves 4

4 peaches

750ml sauternes

½ vanilla pod, split lengthways

2 slices lemon

120g caster sugar

2 egg yolks

50ml cream

1 tbsp amandine (French almond liqueur)

To serve

icing sugar, for dusting

4 scoops almond ice cream (page 215)

To prepare the peaches, bring a large saucepan of water to the boil and get a bowl of cold water ready. Immerse the peaches in the boiling water, count to ten, then remove them and place in the cold water. Carefully peel away the skins.

Discard the hot water and combine the sauternes, split vanilla pod, lemon slices and sugar in the saucepan. Add the peeled peaches. Bring to the boil then turn the heat down so that the liquid simmers. Cover with a large circle of greaseproof paper and a lid and poach for 5 minutes.

Remove the pan from the heat and allow the peaches to cool in the syrup.

Once the peaches have cooled, lift them from the syrup and set aside. Measure 300ml of the syrup and put it in a saucepan. Bring to the boil over a high heat and let the syrup bubble away so that it reduces to 100ml in volume.

Put the egg yolks in a bowl and pour the hot peach syrup over them, whisking continuously to give a thick, light mixture.

Whip the cream until soft peaks form then fold it into the egg mixture along with the amandine.

Preheat the grill to the highest setting. Cut the peaches into thick slices and spread them out evenly on heatproof serving plates.

Spoon the sabayon over the fruit. Dust with icing sugar and grill until evenly brown. Serve with a scoop of almond ice cream.

The pistachio paste needed for Angela's stunning soufflé is easiest to find in speciality Italian delicatessens or online, but as it is quite pricey you may want to keep this recipe for special occasions. Similar blends of hazelnuts and almonds are available, and you could use these instead if necessary. This is delicious served with bitter chocolate sauce, or a chocolate sorbet, says Angela. For a slick finish, try hiding some roasted pistachios in the bottom of each ramekin for a surprise crunch.

pistachio souffle

✳ ✳ ✳

Serves 4-6

600ml milk

1 vanilla pod, split and seeds scraped

180g caster sugar

80g flour

4 egg yolks and 160g egg whites

300g pistachio paste

60g butter

100g chocolate, grated and well chilled

icing sugar, to finish

Bring the milk, vanilla pod and seeds, and 30g of the sugar slowly to the boil in a saucepan.

Meanwhile, in a mixing bowl, rub together the flour and butter until the mixture resembles fine breadcrumbs, then stir in 90g of the sugar.

When the milk has reached boiling point, tip the flour mixture into it and cook over a low heat, whisking all the time.

Remove the saucepan from the heat and allow to cool before mixing in the egg yolks. Pass the mixture through a sieve into a bowl, then stir in the pistachio paste.

Preheat the oven to 180°C/gas 4. Rub the inside of the ramekins liberally with butter, then add the grated chocolate and tap it around to evenly coat the inside. Tip the chocolate from one ramekin to the other as they are coated.

In a large bowl, whisk the egg whites and the remaining 60g sugar together to make a meringue. Keep whisking until stiff peaks form when the whisk is lifted from the meringue.

Measure 130g of the pistachio mixture and fold it gently into the meringue.

Carefully spoon the mixture into the lined ramekins and smooth over the surface with a palette knife. Bake for 5-7 minutes, until the soufflés have risen. Serve immediately, dusted with icing sugar.

Relax! Choux is one of the easiest pastries to make, says John, and can be used for much more than profiteroles. Don't restrict its use to puddings either: it is delicious flavoured with cheese, or made into savoury fritters.

choux pastry *for profiteroles*

Makes about 60
260ml milk
1 tsp sugar
pinch of salt
100g butter, diced
120g plain flour
4 eggs

Quickly sieve in the flour and whisk it into the liquid ingredients.

Combine the milk, sugar, salt and diced butter in a heavy-based saucepan. Heat gently until the butter has melted.

Still over a low heat, beat the ingredients vigorously together for about 5 minutes.

In a mixing bowl, beat the eggs together thoroughly, you want no strings of white when it hits the hot paste. Slowly, in three or more batches, beat the eggs into the paste.

Pipe balls the size of a 50p coin on baking sheets lined with silicone paper, or greased baking trays.

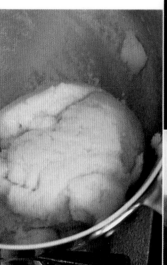

The paste is ready for the next stage when it clumps together in a smooth ball and comes cleanly from the sides of the pan. Remove from the heat and allow to cool.

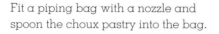

Fit a piping bag with a nozzle and spoon the choux pastry into the bag.

Bake in batches in an oven preheated to 220°C/gas 7 for 20-25 minutes, or until golden brown and crisp (if just yellow they will deflate on cooling). When they are done, the inside should be hollow. Tip them on to a wire rack to cool.

Far from being a '70s throwback, profiteroles are an enduringly popular dessert welcome any time they are placed on the table. Here John gives a choice of light cream fillings. He favours the Valrhona brand of chocolate from France and insists that choosing a quality brand makes a great difference to the result. However, he says there is no need to seek out very bitter varieties with a cocoa solids content of higher than 80 per cent. One that is 70 per cent cocoa solids or thereabouts will be perfect.

profiteroles *with vanilla cream*

Makes about 30 (serves 6)
½ recipe quantity choux buns (see previous pages)
150g chocolate (see above)

For the vanilla cream
150ml double cream
1 tbsp icing sugar
1 vanilla pod, split and seeds scraped out

If you have not already done so, bake the choux buns as described on the previous page.

To make the vanilla cream, pour the double cream into a large bowl and add the icing sugar and vanilla seeds. Whip until the mixture forms soft peaks when the whisk is lifted from the bowl.

Melt the chocolate in a heatproof bowl over a pan of steaming hot water, being careful not to overheat it.

Spoon the vanilla cream into a piping bag and set aside.

With the tip of a knife, make a small hole in each choux bun. Gently fill each bun with the vanilla cream by placing the nozzle in the hole you have cut and squeezing the piping bag so that the cream flows into the bun.

Carefully dip the top of each filled bun into the melted chocolate and allow it to set before serving.

Variations For an orange-flavoured cream that tastes delicious with dark chocolate, replace the seeds of the vanilla pod with the finely grated zest of one orange. The traditional French filling is crème patissière. To make it bring 300ml milk to the boil with half a vanilla pod. In a mixing bowl whisk 3 egg yolks with 30g cornflour and 60g caster sugar. Pour the hot milk on to the egg mixture, then return the custard to the saucepan and bring to the boil, whisking continuously. Leave to cool before using.

Much more than something to serve with coffee after dinner, you will save a fortune on Christmas presents with this recipe, says John. Put your home-made truffles in a box, wrap them nicely, and your friends and family will be delighted, for they are much better than the chocolates you find on sale in shops. The ganache (the chocolate and cream mixture that forms the centre of the truffle) is sweetened with honey and orange liqueur. Coat them in whatever you fancy – cocoa powder, icing sugar or chocolate sprinkles.

chocolate truffles

Makes about 30

400g dark chocolate

30g clear honey

25g unsalted butter

200ml double cream

3 tbsp cointreau

icing sugar, cocoa powder or chocolate vermicelli, for dusting

Chop the chocolate and place 300g of it in a mixing bowl.

In a saucepan, combine the honey, butter, cream and cointreau, and bring to the boil. Pour the mixture into the bowl, stirring until the chocolate has melted and is smooth. Place in the refrigerator for 45 minutes to 1 hour to chill.

Using a melon baller, scoop out balls of the chocolate to make truffles and place on a sheet of greaseproof paper.

Melt the remaining 100g chopped chocolate in a bowl set over a pan of steaming hot water. Remove from the heat.

Put the icing sugar, cocoa powder or vermicelli in a dish.

Dip the truffles one at a time in the chocolate and allow to set.

Roll each truffle in the icing sugar, cocoa powder or vermicelli until evenly coated. Store in the refrigerator for up to a week.

Everyone loves chocolate mousse, says John. But why do people persist in buying poor examples from the supermarket when it is so easy to make? Not only does this recipe taste more delicious that ready-made mousses, you have the advantage of knowing all the ingredients. He suggests using a chocolate with a high cocoa solids content for the best flavour, but that is not the only indicator of quality: fine bars of chocolate also have a high shine and break with a sharp snap. Choose the best you can afford.

chocolate mousse

Serves 4

65g good-quality chocolate, at least 75 per cent cocoa solids

2 tbsp sugar syrup (see page 207)

3 egg yolks

125ml double cream

Place a heatproof bowl over a pan of gently simmering water. Break up the chocolate and put it in the bowl. Stir until completely melted, then take it off the heat and leave to one side.

Meanwhile, heat the sugar syrup in a small pan.

Put the egg yolks in a mixing bowl. Pour the hot sugar syrup over them, whisking constantly, until the mixture turns pale and thickens.

Pour the melted chocolate into the egg mixture. Lightly whip the double cream and fold it into the chocolate mixture.

Divide the mousse among serving glasses and chill for several hours or overnight before serving.

Variation To dress the mousse up for a dinner party, top with some chantilly cream and decorate with some colourful berry fruit.

Chocolate, pistachio and vanilla ice cream all go well with John's rich, silky-textured fondant, but you could also serve it with a little whipped cream or a frothy custard sauce drizzled around the plate. This is the perfect pudding for a dinner party – not only can it be prepared well in advance, you need not serve it straight from the oven. In fact, it is best served warm rather than hot.

hot chocolate & coffee fondant

Serves 4

175g plain chocolate

175g unsalted butter, plus extra for greasing

4 whole eggs, plus 4 eggs yolks

50g instant coffee powder

75g caster sugar

75g plain flour

icing sugar, for dusting

ice cream, whipped cream, or crème anglaise, to serve

Tip
Don't try to cook the fondant straight away. The mixture has to firm up in the cold of the fridge so that when it's baked the interior stays deliciously gooey.

Quarter fill a saucepan with water and bring it to a low simmer.

Cut the chocolate and butter into small pieces and put them in a heatproof bowl that will sit over the steaming water. Allow them to melt together gently over the heat.

Remove the bowl from the pan and whisk the four egg yolks into the chocolate mixture. Set aside to cool.

In a separate bowl, combine the whole eggs, coffee powder, sugar and flour, and mix until smooth.

When the chocolate mixture has cooled, fold it into the coffee mixture.

Grease four ramekins with butter and spoon the fondant mixture in so that they are about three-quarters full. Chill for at least half an hour, preferably more.

Preheat the oven to 200°C/gas 6. Bake the fondants for 8-9 minutes.

Run a knife around the rim of the ramekins to loosen the fondants and turn them out carefully on to serving plates. Dust with a little icing sugar and serve warm with ice cream, whipped cream or crème anglaise.

This lovely gooey, chocolatey concoction is the perfect dessert for big kids, says John. It contrasts a soft moussey filling with a sponge finger shell and has a dash of liqueur for a boozy kick. Although it is more straightforward to produce than it perhaps appears, there are a few tricks to getting it right, such as making sure that the top of the charlotte rises above the tin to help it hold its shape. When it comes to serving, less is more as it is very rich, but you could add some ice cream or hot chocolate sauce if desired.

chocolate charlotte

Serves 6-8

For the sponge fingers
3 eggs, separated
90g caster sugar
30g plain flour
30g cornflour
icing sugar, for dusting
Tia Maria liqueur, for brushing

For the filling
240g dark chocolate
4 egg yolks
70g sugar
500ml whipping cream

To decorate
1 recipe quantity chocolate mousse mixture, unchilled (page 244)
icing sugar, for dusting
chocolate flakes, for sprinkling

Tip
Try to pipe the sponge fingers so that they're touching each other. Then, after baking, the whole lot can be removed in a single sheet, to cleverly line the spring-form tin in one go.

First make the sponge fingers: preheat the oven to 220°C/gas 7, in a mixing bowl, whisk together the egg yolks and 60g caster sugar until the mixture is pale and thick.

Using a clean whisk and another large bowl, whisk the egg whites until they form stiff peaks. Add the remaining 30g caster sugar and whisk to combine. Gently fold the egg whites into the yolk mixture.

Sieve the flour and cornflour over the egg mixture, then gently fold until the ingredients are well mixed.

Lay a sheet of silicone paper on a baking sheet. Put the sponge mixture in a piping bag fitted with a nozzle and pipe fingers 1cm wide and 5cm long onto the silicone paper.

Dust the sponge fingers generously with icing sugar then bake for 5-6 minutes. Remove from the oven and set aside to cool on a wire rack.

Once they have cooled, take a 20cm spring-form cake tin and use the sponge fingers to line the sides, trimming them if necessary. Dab with the Tia Maria.

To make the filling, chop the chocolate and melt it in a bowl set over a pan of simmering water. In a separate pan, combine the sugar and 120ml water and bring to the boil, stirring until the sugar has dissolved. Remove this syrup from the heat.

Set a heatproof bowl over a pan of simmering water. Put the egg yolks and 120ml of the syrup in it and, using an electric whisk, whisk over the heat until the mixture is thick and white. Remove from the heat.

Whip the cream until stiff peaks form.

Fold the melted chocolate into the yolk mixture, then fold in the whipped cream, being careful not to over-mix. Pour into the lined cake tin. Smooth over the top and allow to set.

To decorate, put the chocolate mousse mixture in a piping bag fitted with a suitable nozzle and pipe it decoratively across the top of the set chocolate filling.

Carefully remove the sides of the tin, dust with icing sugar and scatter with a few chocolate curls on top before serving, cut into portions with a warm knife.

index

Authors' acknowledgements

John Burton Race would like to give a special thank-you to his partner in crime, Angela Hartnett. Big thank-yous, too, to his head chef Robert Spencer, for all his hard work and support, and to all the boys in The New Angel kitchen - Jim, Malcom, Phil (aka Gordon!), Steve and Julien, and restaurant manager, Jean Bertrand de March. John's thanks go also to his PA Penny Spencer for the endless typing, and Bo Steer and Elaine Ashton of Creative Talent Ltd for their support.

Angela Hartnett would like to thank John Burton Race, as well as Diego Cardoso, head chef at the Connaught, for all his help and organisation; and restaurant manager Yishay Malkov.

Both authors would like to thank Pat Llewellyn, Ben Adler, Paul Ratcliffe, Paul Berczeller and Nicola Moody of Optomen, and the fantastic crew that worked so hard putting the programme together: Richard Hill, Derek Bruce, Rafick Affejee, Stuart Clayton and Mike Sarah, also Shelley Gale and Alex Croxford in production and Jo Ogden. Special thanks to home economists Lisa Harrison and Karen Taylor for their patient assistance. And last but by no means least, all the 'criminals' who took part and entertained us,

Also Anne Furniss of Quadrille, art director Gabriella Le Grazie, photographer Peter Cassidy and editors Jenni Muir and Lewis Esson for transferring TV to book so professionally.

First published in 2007 by

Quadrille Publishing Limited
Alhambra House
27-31 Charing Cross Road,
London WC2H OLS

Editorial Director: *Anne Furniss*
Creative Director: *Helen Lewis*
Art Director: *Gabriella Le Grazie*
Project Editor: *Jenni Muir*
Editor: *Lewis Esson*
Photography: *Peter Cassidy*
Styling: *Liz Belton*
Additional food styling: *Annie Rigg*
Production: *Bridget Fish, Vincent Smith*

Optomen Television:
Managing Director: *Patricia Llewellyn*
Executive Producer: *Nicola Moody*
Series Producer: *Paul Ratcliffe*
Series Director: *Paul Berczeller*
Researcher: *Joanna Ogden*
Food Stylist: *Lisa Harrison*

optomen

Optomen Television Limited
1 Valentine Place
London SE1 8QH
www.optomen.com

Cataloguing in Publication Data: a catalogue record for this book is available from the British Library

ISBN 978 184400 5215

Printed and bound in Germany